THE KNIGHTS TEMPLARS

God's Warriors, the Devil's Bankers

Frank Sanello

TAYLOR TRADE PUBLISHING

Lanham New York • Oxford

First Taylor Trade Publishing edition 2003

This Taylor Trade Publishing hardcover edition of *The Knights Templar* is an original publication. It is published by arrangement with the author.

Published by Taylor Trade Publishing
A Member of the Rowman & Littlefield Publishing Group
4501 Forbes Boulevard, Suite 200
Lanham, Maryland 20706

Distributed by National Book Network

Library of Congress Cataloging-in-Publication Data

Sanello, Frank.
    The Knights Templars : God's warriors, the devil's bankers / Frank Sanello.
        p. cm.
    Includes bibliographical references (p. 289) and index.
    ISBN 0-87833-302-9 (alk. paper)
    1. Templars—History. I. Title.
CR4743 .S3 2003
271'.7913—dc21   2003006714

♾™ The paper used in this publication meets the minimum requirements of American National Standard for Information Sciences—Permanence of Paper for Printed Library Materials, ANSI/NISO Z39.48–1992.
Manufactured in the United States of America.

For Bryan Smith

CONTENTS

PART ONE

Palestine

Jerusalem, indeed all of the Holy Land, was a terrifying place, not unlike our own Wild West, when Hugues de Payen, a veteran of the Crusades, showed up there in the early years of the twelfth century. The capital was a city perpetually under siege by guerilla attack, except, unlike in our Old West, the local marauders were not Stone Age hunter-gatherers but dispossessed members of a more advanced civilization and culture—also better armed and equipped than the besieged occupiers of their homeland.

The Order of the Poor Knights of Christ and the Temple of Solomon was founded by de Payen, a knight who had fought in the First Crusade and participated in the capture of Jerusalem. De Payen was a member of the minor nobility and a vassal of a powerful feudal magnate, the Count of Champagne.

On a date lost to history in the year 1118 A.D., de Payen and eight comrades, unsolicited, presented themselves at the palace of Baldwin I, the King of Jerusalem. Baldwin's late brother, Godfrey of Bouillon, had taken the city from the Saracens nineteen years earlier. The Patriarch of Jerusalem was also present at the meeting. Both the secular and religious leaders greeted de Payen and his men warmly. The King, in fact, placed an entire wing of his palace at their disposal and provided funds for their upkeep. Their new quarters rested on the ruins of a desecrated Arab mosque under which lay the remains of the ancient Temple of Solomon, the origin of the new order's name, Templars. The first of many legends surrounding the Templars began at this site, which the knights reportedly spent ten years excavating after gaining possession of it in hopes of finding the Holy Grail, the mythical cup of Jesus' Last Supper. Conspiracy buffs, but not legitimate historians, maintain that the Templars were successful in their search, and that the Holy Grail was one of the order's most prized treasures, disappearing with the rest of its fabled wealth when the Templars were outlawed two centuries later.

Besides excavating the site, the Templars changed the façade and interior of the Temple to reflect the order's military role. The new Temple of Solomon anticipated Mies van der Rohe's famous dictum that form follows function by almost a thousand years. The façade of the Temple was festooned with armor and shields. Every square inch of the interior walls displayed the hardware of medieval warfare: bridles, saddles, and lances. The Temple was more armory than monastery, a military barracks more than a temple.

The King of Jerusalem did not object to the Templars' excavation of the sacred site or their less than pious taste for interior decor. In fact, Baldwin was an enthusiastic host because of the novel services de Payen and his comrades offered to perform for the beleaguered monarch.

The knights told the King that their goal was "as far as their strength permitted, they should keep the roads and highways safe . . . with especial regard for protection of pilgrims." The offer was irresistible to the King and the Patriarch. The First Crusade's stated purpose had been to recover Jerusalem so pilgrims could visit Christ's birthplace, which had been forbidden after the Egyptian Saracens had taken the city at the end of the eleventh century.

While the Crusaders had conquered Jerusalem and made the city proper safe, the route to Jerusalem was plagued with bandits, dispossessed Muslims, and terrifying Bedouin horsemen who thundered over from their base camps in Jordan. The Victorian historian Charles G. Addison described the crisis succinctly: "The infidels had indeed been driven out of Jerusalem, but not out of Palestine." Pilgrims disembarking at the port of Jaffa had to make their way inland to Jerusalem while enduring a perilous gauntlet that also included attacks by wild animals. The King may have been especially receptive to the Templars' offer of protection since he himself had once been a prisoner of the Saracens.

In a ceremony at the Church of the Resurrection in Jerusalem, with the Patriarch presiding, the knights transformed themselves into monks and swore vows of chastity, obedience, and poverty. Eventually, it would be a matter of debate and murderous accusations exactly to whom the Templars owed obedience. As for their vow of poverty, the Church at this time conveniently recognized three forms of poverty: the first and strictest forbade the possession of all goods and property; the second prohibited the individual from owning property but allowed wealth to be shared by the group to which the individual belonged; the third accepted individual possession of food and clothing, with all other goods shared in common. The Templars adopted the second form, which would allow them to become enormously wealthy despite their vow of poverty, which was elastic.

At the beginning of the twelfth century, the Holy Land was more scary than holy. Why had Jerusalem been recovered at the cost of so many lives and expense if pilgrims couldn't reach the Holy Places within the city?

Financially and physically exhausted by the war to recapture the Holy Land and deserted by many Crusaders who returned to Europe with plunder once the city had been liberated, King Baldwin found himself undermanned, underfinanced, and outgunned to complete the work of the First Crusade—that is, to provide safe access to his capital. The Templars filled this vacuum as bodyguards consecrated by the church for the protection of pilgrims.

Despite their official name, The Order of the Poor Knights of Christ and the Temple of Solomon, the founding members were anything but poor. Many belonged to some of the most prominent aristocratic families in France and Flanders. As their fame in the Holy Land filtered back to Europe via breathless accounts of chroniclers who served as publicists for the Templars, many prominent rulers and noblemen joined the order as lay brothers. One of them, Fulk, Count of Anjou, added to the Templars' wealth with the annual gift of thirty pounds of silver. Membership among the laity became so fashionable that Hugues de

PIOUS AND FIERCE: Although this armed figure looks like a typical medieval knight, he was also a monk who took vows of chastity, poverty, and obedience as a member of the Knights Templars, originally a group of French aristocrats who served during the Crusades as protectors of pilgrims visiting the Holy Places in Jerusalem.

Payen's overlord, the Count of Champagne, submitted to his former vassal and joined the order as a lay member in 1123.

King Baldwin of Jerusalem, valuing their military services, became the order's biggest booster and sent two Templars back to Europe to secure papal approval and recruit more knight-protectors for his besieged kingdom. In 1127, with the blessing of the Patriarch of Jerusalem, Baldwin sent Templars Andrew and Gondemar to Hugues de Payen's homeland in the Champagne region of France. The knights carried with them a letter from Baldwin to the most famous orator of the age, St. Bernard, the abbot of Clairvaux in France. The letter asked the powerful prelate to use his influence to get official recognition of the order from the Pope and, perhaps more important, a cash grant from the Pontiff. There is something of a whiff of panic in Baldwin's flowery prose when he asks Bernard "to dispose His Holiness to send succor and *subsidies* against the enemies of the Faith, reunited in their design to destroy us and to invade our Christian territories."

The nervous King of Jerusalem redoubled his efforts and sent Hugues de Payen himself, along with five other Templars, to call on the Pope in Rome. Pope Honorius was delighted with this new amalgam of the sacred and profane, holy men who killed in the name of Jesus, and received de Payen and his party with great honor.

In the meantime, Bernard kept himself busy by organizing the Council of Troyes in 1128, at which the order was officially recognized by the Pope and incorporated as a religious-military order with de Payen given the title of Grand Master. The council was an ecclesiastical gala, with all the prominent churchmen of France in attendance, including several archbishops and bishops.

In their original incarnation, the Templars combined the austere discipline of the monastery with a military zeal approaching fanaticism. They envisioned themselves as warrior-monks, soldier-mystics, a "militia of Christ."

St. Bernard accepted Baldwin's brief and became the Templars most powerful proponent. He composed a stirring religious tract, *De Laude Novae Militiae* (In Praise of the New Knighthood), which served as a call to arms and recruitment poster. The tract countered criticism that fighting for any purpose, no matter how noble the cause, was sinful. St. Bernard's work represented an act of absolution, although to the modern reader his argument resembles Orwellian doublespeak: in one passage, the abbot condemns killing, and in the next, he gives the Templars a sacred license to kill. It was the motivation or mindset of the killer that would lead to perdition or paradise, and in the tract's second chapter, Bernard explained the sophist-like difference. Bernard commanded the new order not to "provoketh war or awakeneth strife, either in an irrational impulse of anger or an insane lust of glory, or the covetous desire of possessing another man's lands and possessions. In such causes it is neither safe to slay nor to be slain." In the next chapter, however, he gives the warrior-monks *carte blanche* to kill for Christ. "But the soldiers of Christ indeed securely fight the battles of their Lord, in no wise fearing sin either from the slaughter of the enemy, or danger from their own death. When indeed death is to be given or received for Christ, it has nothing of crime in it, but much glory."

Bernard also composed the Templars' charter, which contained rules of conduct similar to the Cistercians, the monastic order to which Bernard himself belonged.

Like their cloistered counterparts, the Cistercians, the Templars were sworn to poverty, chastity, and obedience. Despite later complaints about their wealth, the charter made it clear that the riches it amassed belonged to the order, not to any individual member. If a knight received a gift of money or land, he was ordered, per the charter, to surrender it at once to the Grand Master.

Over the centuries, the institution became rich, but the membership remained if not poor, at least ascetic, especially in comparison to the lavish lifestyles of other monastic orders.

As a further sign of their otherworldliness, the Templars were forbidden to shave in an era when laymen were clean-shaven. They were also ordered to wear their hair close-cropped at a time when free-flowing locks were the fashion. "It is not seemly in a man to have long hair," St. Bernard wrote in his tract. Their detractors would later claim—inaccurately—that the Templars' vows also forbade bathing! The accusation, however, was not completely unfounded. Bernard described the Templars' grooming habits: "They are never combed, *seldom washed,* but appear rather with rough neglected hair, foul with dust, and with skins browned by the sun and their coats of mail." Among the medieval upper crust, suntans were *declassé*, endured only by peasants who were forced to work in the fields under a blazing sun for centuries before the introduction of sunblock. The Templars' unfashionable tan would add to the mortification of the flesh.

Bernard's charter contained an elegant but oxymoronic combination of the martial and the monastic life, exhorting the Templars to "put on the armour of obedience and associate themselves together with piety and humility for the defense of the Holy Catholic Church ... to employ a pure diligence and a steady perseverance in the exercise of their sacred profession, so that they might share in the happy destiny reserved for the holy warriors who had given up their lives for Christ." This was sanctity at sword-point. When the monks were not on the battlefield, they were supposed to be in church. Bernard's rule ordered "severe devotional exercises, self-mortification, fasting and prayer and a constant attendance at matins, vespers and all other services of the church, so that being refreshed with heavenly food, none might be afraid of the *fight*."

The contemplative duties of the monks had a practical purpose. Meditation gave them focus; prayer made them better fighters. Bernard's charter included other rules that separated the monks from the corrupting influences of the secular world. Letters from friends and families were forbidden. Women were not allowed on the premises, and Bernard made a special point of ordering them to "shun feminine kisses." His exhaustive, anal-retentive charter contained seventy-two clauses and governed the lives of the Templars down to the minutest detail. Silence during dinner, meat only three days a week, and on meatless days only three kinds of vegetables. Bernard was such a micro-manager that even gossip was forbidden in one of the charter's clauses. Nostalgic discussions of the monks' sexual exploits in the past were also proscribed. "It shall not be permitted him to speak . . . of the delight of the flesh with miserable women . . . and we resolutely condemn all tales related by any brother of the follies and irregularities of which he hath been guilty in the world."

The dress code was just as restrictive. The warrior-monks were not allowed to adorn their armor with gold or silver. If they received gifts of armor already decorated with precious metals, they were to paint them black "so that its splendour and beauty may not impart to the wearer an appearance of arrogance beyond his fellows." Besides the spiritual benefit of self-denial, there was a practical reason for the ban on gilded armor. St. Bernard explained that a greedy enemy would be more likely to attack a knight equipped with valuable armor rather than one protected by cheap steel. "On the approach of battle, they fortify themselves with faith within, and with steel without, and not with gold, so that armed and not adorned, they may strike terror into the enemy, rather than awaken his lust of plunder."

For less explicable reasons, members were not allowed to wear animal skins, except those of lamb or rams. Knights had to wear white all year round, while their squires wore black. If black clothing could not be obtained, the almost as unfashionable color brown or a "meaner color" could be substituted. Each knight was allowed a sole squire, but he could maintain three horses. The generous allotment of costly mounts probably reflected the knight's primary function as warrior. Squires who served without pay were not allowed to be beaten by their masters. Bernard's charter implied that salaried squires had to tolerate physical abuse.

The Templars' white monk's robe evolved into a white mantle. In 1146, by order of Pope Eugenius, the red cross of the Crusader was emblazoned on the left breast of the garment so that the Templars could be identified by their Christian allies in battle. The Pope did not seem to realize that the cross would also serve as a bull's-eye for the enemy's arrows and lances.

According to their charter, if a Templar was captured, he was not allowed to ask for mercy or ransom and was expected to fight to the death. However, as the order grew in power and influence, the Templars' sense of self-worth grew commensurately, and they allowed themselves to be ransomed like any other wealthy nobleman or prince.

Falconry, a hunting sport that was an obsession among the medieval aristocracy much like golf is among businessmen today, was also prohibited in the Templars' joyless lives. Recreational hunting with the longbow and crossbow was proscribed because they should be reserved for the sole "purpose of protecting him from the perfidious infidel." Despite a life of bleak asceticism enumerated in the charter, Bernard left one giant loophole among the Puritanical taboos, one that would enrich the Templars but ultimately lead to their destruction. Clause 51 described the unique character of the organization, "the union of warfare with religion, so that religion, being armed, maketh her way by the sword, and smiteth the enemy without sin." In order to accomplish this sacred but contradictory mission, Bernard declared, "Ye ought to have lands." With that simple exhortation, Bernard allowed the Templars to become major landowners in the Christian world. They would be poor in spirit and creature comforts but rich in real estate, with extensive properties stretching from the far north of Scotland all the way to the Crusader castles of Palestine.

In 1139, Pope Innocent II issued the Papal Bull, *Omne Datum Optimum*, which declared that the Templars answered to no one but the Pope himself. They therefore were not under the jurisdiction of any other religious or secular authority. The Templars were independent of all kings, princes, and bishops, which fueled the jealousy and animosity between the order and the local authorities who resented this "Kingdom within a Kingdom." Like the Jesuits centuries later, the

Templars were the Pope's soldiers, autonomous, a law unto themselves. Moreover, like the Jesuits, they would one day be suppressed.

With the blessing and prestige of the papacy behind it, the order grew rapidly in fame and numbers—and wealth. In 1128, Hugues de Payen visited Henry I in England, where he was received with great honor. Like the Crusades, the Templars were a magnet for younger sons of noble families who lacked land and money. They flocked to the order, whether out of piety or a desire to create their own inheritance. With no sense of irony or hypocrisy, these second sons took a vow of poverty upon entering the order and signed over what little property they had to the Templars. The more cynical among them no doubt planned to recoup their losses with plunder and booty amassed in the Holy Land, then resign from the order and retire to their new estates.

In an age where gifts of land and money to charitable institutions served as "after-life insurance," guaranteeing entry into heaven, donations to the Templars poured in from all over Christendom. The will of virtually every grandee included a gift to the Templars. To further ease their entry into heaven, nobles often took the Templars' vows on their deathbed, which allowed them the extra perk of being buried in the Templars' fashionable white mantle.

Within a year of the order's founding at the Council of Troyes, these bequests had made the Templars immensely rich. The order received substantial estates in France, England, Scotland, Flanders, Spain, and Portugal. King Stephen of England donated the vast English manor of Cressing. In Spain, the Templars joined the fight against Muslims under the leadership of Christian kings who were reconquering Spain from the Moors. King Alfonso of Aragon in Northern Spain esteemed the Templars' military contribution to the *Reconquista* so highly that on his death in 1133 he bequeathed his entire kingdom to the order! The Templars were unable to claim their prize, however, because the dead King's vassals refused to honor his will, although they ended up giving the order generous estates in Aragon. (It was also fashionable for kings and princes while still alive and well to symbolically hand over their realms to the Templars while maintaining physical possession. A gift to the Templars also served as a face-saving ploy for a ruler to avoid going on Crusade himself. The Holy Roman Emperor Lothaire, however, took his gift giving more seriously and handed over a huge portion of his empire while he was still alive.)

A decade after the Council of Troyes, the knights had enthusiastically embraced Clause 51 in St. Bernard's charter. The now ironically named Order of the *Poor Knights* of Christ held territory in Italy, Austria, Germany, Hungary, and the Holy Land. It is estimated that at the height of their wealth and power, the Templars owned 9,000 castles and manor houses. Their estimated annual income in Europe alone was six million pounds sterling! Despite the individual knight's vow of poverty, the order's curious charter forbade it from sharing these donations with other charities.

Concubinage in monasteries, one of the scandals that prompted Luther to launch the Protestant Reformation four centuries later, was already an international embarrassment at the time of the Templars' founding. Abbots and their subordinates lived openly with mistresses on monastery grounds. To prevent the practice from infecting the Templars, they were not allowed to accept nuns as members—a unique prohibition among monastic orders of the age. "It is moreover exceedingly dangerous to join sisters with you in your holy profession, for the ancient enemy hath drawn many away from the right path to paradise through the society of women," St. Bernard wrote.

Second sons of noblemen without an inheritance were often dumped in monasteries during childhood, which created another medieval scandal—highborn child abbots and prioresses. To avoid that abuse, the

Templars' charter mandated that children destined for the monastic life were to be raised at home and admitted to the order only after they had reached adulthood. The average Templar recruit was in his mid-twenties. St. Bernard demonstrated a modern knowledge of psychology when he explained why children needed to experience the real world before renouncing it. "For it is better not to vow in childhood, lest afterwards the grown man should foully fall away."

Considering their later reputation for arrogance and pride, it was ironic that one clause declared that if a boastful member refused to change his behavior after repeated warnings, he should be expelled from the order. "If by godly admonition and earnest reasoning he will not be amended, but will go on more and more lifting himself up with pride, then let him be cast out of the flock." In a grim reversal of the story of the Old Testament's Prodigal Son, Bernard wrote, "It is necessary that from the society of the Faithful Brothers the dying sheep be removed."

Not all those who joined the Templars were penurious second sons of noblemen seeking to create their own patrimony. Wealthy but idealistic aristocrats also sought out the monastic life. When they entered the order, the nobles surrendered all their property and lands, another reason the Templars rapidly accumulated wealth.

A prestigious pedigree, however, was no guarantee of admission to the order. Aspirants had to prove themselves by deeds, not birth. A good example was the powerful Hugh d'Amboise, who governed large areas of France. Hugh was accused of overtaxing his subjects and ignored the orders of his overlord, the Count of Anjou, to stop the abuse. When Hugh asked to join the Templars, they turned him down until he repented in public and returned the taxes he had extorted.

Yet another reason for their growing prosperity was the fact that as a charitable organization, the Templars paid no taxes, which further antagonized the rulers of the countries in which the monks formed a country within a country.

Armed with St. Bernard's charter, the Pope's blessing, and a huge contingent of knights who joined the order during Hugues de Payen's trip to Europe, the Grand Master returned in triumph to Jerusalem, where he was again feted by the grateful King and the Patriarch of Jerusalem. A large council assembled, at which the King and the Templars mapped out strategies for keeping the Muslims at bay. Unfortunately, de Payen died soon after his return to the Holy Land in 1136. Reflecting the increased prestige of the order, the new Grand Master, Robert of Burgundy, came from a more prominent family than de Payen, and was the son-in-law of

Anselm, Archbishop of Canterbury. Like many other newcomers to the order, Robert was a recent widower who decided not to remarry and instead took the Templar vow of chastity. The new Grand Master's military skills, however, were inferior to his pedigree, and during his ten-year tenure, a series of defeats suffered by the Christian forces dramatically shrank the kingdom of Jerusalem.

Under attack by two powerful Muslim generals, Emod-ed-deen and Nour-ed-deen, the Christians lost the crucial port city of Edessa and the fortified castles of Arlene, Mamoula, Basarfont, and Kafarlatha. Fearing the loss of the capital itself, the King sent emissaries pleading for reinforcements to Rome, where the Pope ordered St. Bernard to preach the Second Crusade. The incompetent Robert of Burgundy died at this time and was replaced in 1146 by Everard des Barres, the former Prior of France, who called a grand council in Paris attended by Pope Eugenius III, King Louis VII of France, and a who's who of religious and secular notables from across Western Europe. The gathering turned into a war council where the strategy of the Second Crusade was mapped out. The event also served as a successful charity drive, as great magnates vied with one another to make land grants to support the Templars in prosecuting the new Crusade. Bernard

Baliol bequeathed his castle at Wedelee, which became the Templars' headquarters in England. Even grander nobles like the Dukes of Brittany and Lorraine and the Counts of Brabant and Fourcalquier contributed vast estates, whose revenues would finance the Crusade.

In 1146, the new Grand Master, Everard des Barres, accompanied by the King of France, set out for the Holy Land with the cream of European nobility in tow. During the dangerous march through Asia Minor (modern day Turkey), the Templars guarded the Crusaders' flanks and distinguished themselves by their bravery, which at times seemed to border on the suicidal. Their courage had an ulterior motive. In the Middle Ages, entering a monastery was widely considered the surest route to heaven. As monks, the Templars felt assured of eternal salvation, which contributed to their zeal as warriors. Death was not a terrifying proposition, since it would lead to paradise. As God's warriors, they felt they were literally fighting their way into heaven. Muslims held a similar belief, which fueled their military success. Mohammed had decreed that any warrior who died fighting for Islam went straight to heaven. This promise of a happy afterlife allowed a small nomadic tribe from the Arabian peninsula to conquer half the known world within a century of Mohammed's death. A similar promise provided much of the impetus for the Crusades, but with less success.

During the dangerous trip to Palestine, King Louis became enamored of the Templars, not only for their bravery, but also for their poverty and humility. In one chronicle, the King's chaplain, Odo of Deuil, wrote that Louis held a council at which he praised the Templars and ordered his secular knights to emulate their behavior. King Louis also fostered the jealousy that would ultimately destroy the Templars by placing them in charge of all his knights.

When the Crusaders finally reached Jerusalem, they found a city in crisis and under siege. The Holy Roman Emperor, Conrad III, had managed to arrive in the Holy Land ahead of the main body of Crusaders with a huge army at his command. But Conrad's soldiers proved no match for the Muslims, who cut his army to pieces before it reached Jerusalem. The Emperor fled to Constantinople, where he boarded a merchant ship and sailed back to Palestine. The Emperor's once-great army was reduced to a few attendants who entered the capital with him. The Templars who had remained in Jerusalem while their master barnstormed Europe for recruits took the desolate Emperor into their Temple and consoled him with lavish entertainment.

Louis and Everard des Barres arrived soon thereafter, and together with Conrad they marched from Jerusalem to Damascus, where they laid siege to the strategic city, which was nicknamed the Queen of Syria. Despite a force of 50,000 men, the Crusaders failed to take the city and retreated to Jerusalem. Despite the embarrassing setback, King Louis again singled out the Templars for praise. But in a curious letter he sent to Abbot Suger of St. Denis, who ruled France in his absence, Louis hinted that his enthusiasm for the Templars was also based on their generosity, which would eventually be extended to royal houses throughout Europe. Louis wrote to his confidant, Abbot Suger, "I cannot imagine how we could have subsisted for even the smallest space of time in these parts had it not been for [the Templars'] support and assistance." Then Louis revealed a more compelling reason for sending his letter. "I have to inform you that they have lent me a considerable sum of money, which must be repaid to them quickly so that I may keep my word . . ." Louis felt only gratitude toward his creditors. Future rulers would come to resent the power of the Templars' purse strings, a resentment that would destroy the order.

Meanwhile, the exploits of the warrior monks filtered back to Europe and resulted in an orgy of landgiving by royalty and nobility. Two English magnates, Roger de Mowbray and William de Warrenne, fought along-side the Templars in Palestine. They were so impressed by their monastic allies that when they returned home they donated not just manors and castles, but entire cities, including Balshall in Warwickshire. King Stephen of England had declined to accompany the Templars on the Second Crusade, but what he lacked in bravery he more than made up for with huge land grants to the Templars. His wife, Queen Mathilda, also enriched the Templars with estates donated in the name of her late father to expedite his passage to heaven.

After his humiliation outside the gates of Damascus, Louis lost enthusiasm for the Second Crusade and returned to France in 1148. He took his favorite knight, the Templars' Grand Master Everard des Barres, with him.

The luckless Templars who remained in the East found themselves leaderless and outnumbered by the enemy. While Everard played royal favorite and courtier in Paris, the order's treasurer in Jerusalem sent the Grand Master a desperate letter, describing their defeats and begging for reinforcements. The treasurer recounted the loss of the critical citadel of Antioch and the death of its ruler in battle. As a sign of how badly the situation had deteriorated since the arrival of a European force num-bering 50,000 soldiers, the treasurer reported that the King of Jerusalem tried to retake Antioch with only

120 knights and 1,000 squires, and soon found their tiny party surrounded by the enemy. From the beleaguered camp, the treasurer's letter was a desperate SOS to Everard at Louis' court: "Overwhelmed with grief at the pitiable condition to which we are reduced, we conjure you to abandon everything and embark [return to Palestine] without delay." The treasurer accurately predicted the loss of the entire Holy Land if the Grand Master did not return and begged him to use his influence with his royal and ecclesiastical cronies to do the same. "It is also of the last importance to announce to the Pope, to the King of France, and to all the princes and prelates of Europe, the approaching desolation of the Holy Land ... come to our rescue; it is from you we await liberty and life!"

Something had happened to the once valiant Everard des Barres after the debacle in Damascus. Upon receipt of his treasurer's letter, instead of orchestrating a new Crusade with the help of his powerful friends, Everard renounced his title and entered the monastery of the order's original patron, Clarivaux, where he ended his days in the unwar-like ways of a traditional monk, engaged in acts of penance and prayer.

Everard's successor had a more impressive résumé and would enjoy greater military success. Bernard de Tremelay came from one of Burgundy's most noble families and had been an accomplished warrior before entering the order. De Tremelay was a proactive leader. When Muslim forces laid siege to Jerusalem, the new Grand Master marched out of the city and attacked the besiegers. De Tremelay not only slaughtered many of the attackers, he pursued the remainder all the way back to their stronghold in Jordan. Five thousand Muslims died in these battles.

The military achievements and fame of the Templars created among their ranks an arrogance condemned in many contemporary chronicles. Their most vociferous critic was the twelfth-century William of Tyre, Archbishop of the City and Chancellor of the Kingdom of Jerusalem. William composed a famous chronicle, *Historia Rerum in Partibus Transmarinis Gestarum*, which blasted the greed of the Templars. In his account of the assault on the city of Ascalon in Palestine in 1153, William wrote that when the Templars breached the walls of the city, they refused to allow any other Crusaders to enter so they could seize all the plunder for themselves. This was not only greed but bad military policy, and the Templars paid dearly for their cupidity. Without the assistance of the other Crusaders, the knights were soon surrounded and the entire force annihilated, including the Grand Master,

VALUED CAPTIVE: Bertrand de Blanquefort, a French knight, was Grand Master of the Templars from 1156 A.D. to 1169 A.D. Captured by the Saracens in Palestine, de Blanquefort was ransomed by the Emperor of Constantinople, who valued the Templars as a well-armed buffer between the encroaching forces of Islam and the decaying Byzantine Empire.

de Tremelay. The victors hung the bodies of the slain Templars from the city's walls.

De Tremelay's successor, Bertrand of Blanquefort, almost suffered the same fate as his predecessor. The Templars always seemed to be engaged in some warlike endeavor, and the decimation of their numbers reflected their reckless courage. While accompanying King Baldwin of Jerusalem on a trip to Tiberias, the Templars were ambushed and 300 of them died in battle while eighty-seven were taken prisoner, among them de Blanquefort. Despite their charter, which forbade paying their ransom, the rule had come to be ignored because of their valuable services and aristocratic rank. De Blanquefort was ransomed for a huge sum, paid for by Manuel Comnenus, the Emperor of Constantinople, who valued the Crusaders in general and the Templars in particular as an important buffer between his empire and the Muslims who encroached on it. As soon as he was released, de Blanquefort wrote a letter to his patron, King Louis VII of France, describing the ferocity of the Muslims, who were capturing town after town in the Holy Land. Adding to the military setbacks, an earthquake had destroyed several Templar fortresses and the walls of other Christian-held cities. De Blanquefort's report wasn't all bad news, however. The Templars had captured the populous and strategic city of Belbeis in Egypt. Unfortunately, while the main force of the Templars was out of the country, the Egyptian general, Nour-ed-deen, invaded Palestine. In a battle with the tiny remnant of Templars, the Egyptians slaughtered sixty of them, leaving the corpses to rot on the plain outside Jerusalem.

Another allegation in William of Tyre's chronicle claimed that the Templars' greed resulted in sacrilege. After they captured an Egyptian nobleman, Nasr-ed-din, he agreed to convert to Christianity in return for his freedom. According to William, Nasr-ed-din learned Latin and was baptized a Christian. An important secondary goal of the Crusades was to convert the infidel, and Nasr-ed-din presented the Templars with the perfect opportunity to lead a nonbeliever to the true faith. Instead, William claimed that for 60,000 pieces of gold, the Templars sold the convert to his Egyptian enemies, who executed him.

Contemporary Arab historians told a different story, which repudiated William of Tyre's accusations. According to these historians, Nasr-ed-din had murdered the Caliph (the religious and temporal ruler) of Egypt, then fled to the Templar fortress at Gaza. The sister of the Caliph wrote to the commander of Gaza, offering a reward for the return of her brother's assassin. The Templars accepted the offer and surrounded

Nasr-ed-din, who according to Arab chroniclers was chopped into tiny pieces by outraged members of the slain Caliph's harem.

The Templars also had defenders among members of their own faith. William's contemporary and adversary, James of Vitry, the Bishop of Acre, a port city on the coast of Palestine, praised the order and claimed they were universally admired for their piety and humility. James wrote, "*Nulli molesti erant sed ab omnibus propater humilitatem et regionem ambantur.*" ("They molested no one, but were loved by all for their humility and devotion to religion.")

The Templars had another, higher placed champion. Pope Alexander III sent letters to archbishops and bishops throughout Europe praising the Templars and asking the prelates to aid them in any way possible. "We implore and admonish your fraternity," Alexander wrote, "that out of love of God, and also out of regard for the salvation of your own souls, ye do favor and support and honor and preserve all their rights entire and intact, and afford them the benefit of your patronage and protection." The Pope's letters again underline a major reason for the continuing popularity of the Templars. Donations to the holy monks helped smooth the donors' way to heaven—or as Alexander stated the reason for supporting the Templars, "for the salvation of your own souls."

Amalric, who succeeded Baldwin as King of Jerusalem, had a more urgent reason to praise the Templars besides their providing after-life insurance. In a letter to Louis VII, he insisted that the Templars were the only reason the Christian kingdom in Palestine remained in existence. "We earnestly entreat your Majesty constantly to extend to the utmost your favour and regard to the brothers of the Temple, who continually render up their lives for God and the faith, and [on] whom is placed the entire reliance of all those in the eastern regions who tread in the right path."

While Amalric valued the services of the Templars, the ambitious ruler failed to heed their advice, which led to the fall of Jerusalem. In 1168, the Christians and the Saracens enjoyed a rare moment of peace after signing a treaty. Amalric decided to abrogate the agreement and invade Egypt for the sole sake of plundering the kingdom whose wealth was legendary. When Amalric asked the Templars' Grand Master, Philip of Nablus, to participate in his corrupt Crusade, Philip not only refused, but also ordered all the Templars under his command to ignore Amalric's invitation. For once, their acerbic critic, William of Tyre, had kind words to say about the monks he loved to hate: "For it appeared a hard matter to the Templars to wage war without cause, in defiance of treaties, and against all honour and conscience, upon a friendly nation, preserving faith with us, and relying on our own faith."

Undaunted, Amalric turned to the Templars' chief rival in the Holy Land, another fighting order of monks known as the Knights Hospitallers. Amalric bribed the Hospitallers' Grand Master, Gilbert d'Assalit, by promising that they could "possess in perpetuity" the wealthy city of Belbeis as reward for their participation in the Egyptian campaign.

Amalric and the Hospitallers captured the undefended city of Belbeis with ease, then massacred the entire population. Even Christian chroniclers were revolted by such unchivalrous behavior by a holy order of monks. The Abbé De Vertot wrote, "They spared neither old men nor women, nor children nursing at the breast." While the attack on Belbeis was a military success, it had a catastrophic result on the entire Christian kingdom of Palestine because Amalric and the Hospitallers' atrocity awoke the sleeping giant who would become known to the world as Saladin.

At the time of the attack, Saladin, the future ruler of Egypt, was an indolent playboy, a Kurdish chieftain who devoted himself to a life of pleasure in the cosmopolitan luxury of Damascus. Upon learning of the massacre at Belbeis, the sybaritic chieftain, a classic late-bloomer, put himself at the head of an army that expelled

Amalric from Egypt. Saladin's forces would one day drive the Christians from all of Palestine. Nineteenth-century historian Charles Addison speculated that Saladin would never have become the scourge of Christendom if Amalric's adventurism had not goaded him to action. "But for the unjustifiable expedition of King Amalric and the Hospitallers against the infidels [in Egypt], the powerful talents and latent energies of the young Kurdish chieftain [Saladin], would in all probability never have been developed."

Two years after the decimation of Belbeis, Saladin felt strong enough to counterattack on the Crusaders' home turf. In 1170, at the head of 40,000 cavalry and infantry, he began to raid the border regions of Palestine. Bedouin horsemen and Arabs from throughout the Middle East flocked to Saladin's colors, and he felt strong enough to lay siege to the Templars' fortress of Gaza, which was considered the key to Jerusalem and the only obstacle to taking the capital. The Templars did not wait for outside help to raise the siege. After a period of prayer and fasting, the Templar army marched out of Gaza and attacked Saladin's army, which was annihilated. The survivors and their commander fled back to their base in Egypt.

News of the great Templar victory made its way back to Europe, where a year after the battle, a grateful

Pope Alexander issued a bull, *Omne Datum Optimum*, which gave the order additional powers and immunities. But these additional favors incited jealousy among the lay and ecclesiastical authorities and contributed to the ultimate destruction of the Templars. In his bull, the Pope exempted the Templars not only from taxation by secular rulers, but secular and religious authorities were forbidden any other power over them. The order was answerable to the Pope alone. In an amazing abdication of his own power, the Pope allowed the Templars to provide religious services, once a year, to individuals and entire countries he had excommunicated. Excommunication was the Pope's most potent weapon. Any country he placed under interdiction (excommunication) damned its citizens to hell if they died before the ban was lifted. But the Pope gave the Templars the right to perform the last rights and save these excommunicants from eternal damnation. In the Middle Ages, when in Hobbes' famous phrase "life was nasty, brutish and short," a happy afterlife was often the only comfort that sustained the miserable faithful.

Less than a decade after the Pope's bull, the favors he had granted the Templars aroused so much resentment that a general council of the Church assembled in Rome, at which the Church hierarchy condemned the Templars' abuse of the Pope's privileges and limited their ability to accept gifts of land or church taxes. The Third Lateran Council claimed that the Templars were using their power to circumvent excommunications more than once a year. The council reiterated that this privilege was to be an annual event. The Council also decreed that the Templars had to the have the approval of the Church before it could receive bequests. They were also forbidden the right to appoint priests to serve the churches that had been bequeathed to them. This was a lucrative privilege because priests paid the Templars a fee for their salaried positions. William of Tyre attended the council in 1179 and reported his enemy's comeuppance in his chronicles with ill-concealed glee.

The Templars may have felt their pride was justified by impressive accomplishments. Besides their fierceness in battle, they demonstrated a singular talent for the more delicate task of diplomacy. They served as arbitrators in disputes among Crusaders, which distracted them from the primary task of freeing and defending Jerusalem. European knights often brought their homegrown feuds along with them to the Holy Land. King Louis VII of France credited the Templars with preventing these internecine squabbles, which had almost destroyed the First Crusade. The Templars kept the warring Crusaders united and ready to fight the common enemy.

Their sphere of operation expanded during the next century from the Holy Land back to Europe, where they became high level diplomats serving kings and nobles.

Brilliant at diplomacy, they managed to enjoy good relations during times of truce with their Saracen enemies. After a generation since their founding, many Templars had been born in Palestine and knew the customs of the country and their enemy well. The Grand Master Philip of Nablus, who headed the order from 1169 to 1171, was a Syrian by birth. Their diplomatic efforts in the Holy Land were aided by the fact that many of the knights spoke fluent Arabic and were experts on local religious cults and sects. This facility explains their unusual and improbable working relationship with the deadly *Hashishim*, or assassins. The *Hashishim* were the Islamic equivalent of the Templars, although more fanatic in their devotion to religion and battle. They pledged blind obedience to their leader, known as "the old man of the mountain," who resisted all attempts at capture by hiding out in the mountains above Tripoli. Masters of disguise, the *Hashishim* carried out assassinations of individuals when larger scale military efforts failed. They accomplished their tasks with the use of a small dagger hidden under voluminous robes called a *hassissin*, a Persian word that gave us the English term for their occupation of assassin. The *Hashishim* paid a monetary tribute to the Templars and were alleged to be in their employ. The Syrian branch of the assassins alone paid the Templars 3,000 gold pieces annually. This financial arrangement added fuel to William of Tyre's obsessive attacks on the order. According to William, the *Hashishim* as a whole asked to convert to Christianity, which would have allowed them to stop paying tribute to the Templars. Unwilling to lose this source of income, the Templars killed the *Hashishim* ambassador on his way to see the King of Jerusalem, where he planned to make the offer to convert.

That was William of Tyre's partisan version of events. Other chroniclers claimed the murder of the ambassador was part of a blood feud that began when a member of the *Hashishim* sect murdered Raymond, the son of the Count of Tripoli, while he was at prayer in the Church of the Blessed Virgin at Tortosa. The Templars were incensed because the murder took place in a holy place. Galvanized by the sacrilege, they succeeded where other Christian warriors had failed, combing the mountains above Tripoli until they captured the elusive "holy man," who agreed to pay an annual tribute of two thousand crowns to the Templars. After they set him free, the holy man, or *imam*, Sinan

Ben Suleiman, sent a member of the sect to Amalric with an offer to embrace Christianity if the Templars released them from paying tribute. Amalric received the ambassador with great honor and sent him back to the *Hashishim* with his consent to the agreement and a bodyguard of Christian knights.

When the ambassador reached the border of Palestine, a detachment of Templars under the command of Walter du Mesnil waylaid the party and killed the *Hashishim* envoy. The outraged King of Jerusalem called a council at Sidon, which ordered Odo de Saint-Amand, the Templars' Grand Master, to surrender the murderer of the envoy, du Mesnil. Odo responded by reminding Amalric that only two years earlier a papal bull had made the Templars answerable to the Pope and no one else. But the Grand Master was an honorable if proud knight, and he did not allow his subordinate to go unpunished. In accordance with papal law, Odo placed du Mesnil in irons and sent him to Rome to be judged by the Pope.

As usual, modern day historians are kinder to the Templars. In the 1950s, Sir Steven Runciman would go no farther than to say the *Hashishim* leader "hinted" he might be open to conversion. By the end of the century, Peter Partner in *The Knights Templar and Their Myth* (1981) was categorical: "It is very unlikely indeed, however, that [the leader] seriously contemplated conversion to Christianity." But Partner is being disingenuous or unfamiliar with human nature when he adds by way of proof that no Muslim chronicles mention the offer to convert, which may have had more to do with Islamic embarrassment rather than lack of documentary evidence. While history remains ambivalent, a timeless consideration of political and religious movements suggests that zealots like the *Hashishim* are the least likely to undergo voluntary conversion.

The Templars continued to thrive in the Holy Land. Twenty years before the *Hashishim* incident, they had been all but annihilated after invading the city of Ascalon. Now, in 1177, in a battle outside the city, they avenged their previous defeat. Two years before the second battle of Ascalon, Saladin, the ruler of Egypt, consolidated his power by assuming control of Damascus upon the death of its sultan. Now Saladin threatened the Holy Land from the north (Syria) and the south (Egypt). His new kingdom supplied additional fighting men, and the sultan assembled an army larger than the Middle East had ever seen: 40,000 infantry, 8,000 mounted knights, and a huge contingent of archers and lancers mounted on dromedaries. Besides these troops, Saladin marched out of his capital, Cairo, with a personal bodyguard of 1,000 slaves turned soldiers called *Mamelukes*.

At the head of this desert armada, the sultan seemed invincible to everyone but the Templars who, under the command of Odo de Saint-Amand, confronted the Islamic host outside Ascalon.

The history of the Crusades and the European presence in Palestine came close to being altered forever during this battle. On November 1, 1177, Odo de Saint-Amand at the head of a mere eighty knights crashed through Saladin's Mameluke bodyguards, killed their leader, and entered Saladin's tent. Humiliated and almost naked, Saladin managed to flee the tent and escaped on a dromedary. Leaderless, the once invincible army of Islam panicked and fled to the desert, where they were pursued by the Christian knights, who slaughtered stragglers but failed to annihilate the main body.

Saladin resurfaced in Damascus, where it took him a year to recover and regroup. In the meantime, the Templars began to build a fortress on the northern frontier of the Latin kingdom, at a place called Jacob's Ford on the River Jordan. Marching down from Damascus, Saladin attacked the Templars, who had not completed work on the citadel, but an army led by the King of Jerusalem beat back Saladin's forces, and the Templars were able to finish construction of the fortress.

Saladin's setback was only temporary, and he resumed the siege of the Templar stronghold after a brief respite. The Templars, the Hospitallers, and secular knights counterattacked in a battle outside the fortress. Saladin's army retreated and the Christians pursued him, but their divided command caused confusion in the ranks. The retreating Saracens rallied and almost annihilated the Christians. The secular leader, the Count of Tripoli, fled to Tyre. The Grand Master of the Hospitallers, after witnessing the slaughter of most of his knights, swam across the River Jordan and sought refuge in the castle of Beaufort. The Templars refused to retreat. Most of them were killed and the rest taken captive, including the Grand Master, Odo de Saint-Amand.

The leaderless Templars inside the fortress resisted Saladin's siege until he set fire to the walls and stormed through an opening. The Muslim chronicler Abulpharadge claimed that the defeated Templars committed suicide en masse. "The Templars flung themselves some into the fire, where they were burned, some cast themselves into the Jordan, some jumped down from the walls on to the rocks and were dashed to pieces. Thus were slain the enemy."

Saladin razed what was left of the citadel. Perhaps in revenge for the humiliation he experienced fleeing his tent after the Templars' attack a year earlier, the sultan ordered the surviving Templars to be sawed in half, sparing only the most senior knights for ransom, according to one chronicle.

Saladin sent Odo de Saint-Armand in chains to Aleppo, where he offered him his freedom in exchange for the sultan's nephew, a captive of the Templars. The Grand Master reiterated the order's vow (often ignored) that Templars never sought ransom and were honor bound to die fighting. Odo told Saladin he only had his saddle and his knife to offer as ransom. Impressed by the Templar's bravery, Saladin spared his life and Odo ended his days in a dungeon in Damascus. Arnold de Torroge left France and assumed the office of Grand Master in Jerusalem.

The Latin kingdom was in crisis. Over the next four years, Saladin ravaged Palestine, burning every city he took, including several Templar fortresses. His troops came as close as a day's march from Jerusalem when the city was saved from almost certain capture in 1184, after rebellions in the north and east of Saladin's empire forced him to abandon his attack on Palestine. Saladin signed a four-year truce with the Christians in return for a huge sum of money while he turned his attention to his rebellious subjects.

The respite galvanized the Christian leaders, who called a council at Jerusalem that sent Heraclius, the city's Patriarch, the Masters of the Temple, and the Hospitallers on a mission to Europe to launch a new Crusade.

The envoys' first target was Henry II, King of England. Henry was the grandson of Fulk, the late King of Jerusalem, and a cousin of its current ruler, Baldwin. The English King had a strong obligation to help the desperate emissaries. He had received absolution for the murder of St. Thomas à Becket, the Archbishop of Canterbury, in return for the promise to go on a Crusade to the Holy Land.

En route to England, the envoys stopped off in Rome, where they received letters from the Pope reminding Henry of his obligations and threatening him with excommunication if he did not comply.

In Verona, Italy, the Templars' Grand Master Arnold de Torroge fell ill and died. The rest of the party continued on to England, where they met the King at Reading. Reflecting the desperate situation in Palestine, the envoys, including the august Patriarch himself, threw themselves weeping at Henry's feet and begged him to save their city. The wily monarch, who had troubles enough of his own at home, put the ambassadors off by promising to bring the subject up at the next meeting of Parliament later that year. Henry was being disingenuous. He did not need the consent of the embryonic, powerless assembly to wage war, but Parliament provided a convenient excuse to delay a Crusade the King did not intend to embark on.

From Reading, the Patriarch of Jerusalem continued on to London, where he stayed at the Templars' monastery. During his visit, the Patriarch consecrated the order's new Temple Church. Heraclius may have felt optimistic about Henry's participation in a new Crusade, since the King had shown the Templars amazing generosity in the past, granting them vast holdings of lands, manors, and churches in both England and Ireland, the latter only recently conquered.

Parliament assembled in April 1185 at the Hospitallers' headquarters at Clerkenwell in London. In addition to English barons and ecclesiastics, the King of Scotland, his brother and many Scottish barons, were also present. The Templars were represented by their new Grand Master, Gerard de Ridefort.

From behind the scenes, Henry choreographed the proceedings and prompted the pliant Parliamentarians to offer creative excuses that would release him from his penance and the trip east to save Jerusalem. Parliament at the end of the twelfth century bore no resemblance to the all-powerful, regicidal monster it would become half a millennium later during the reign of Charles I. Henry's Parliament was not a representative or elective body but an assembly of the landed elite, with the exotic addition of a foreign King [Norman] and *his* elite. It was a rubber-stamp Parliament, which provided Henry with a legal veneer for wriggling out of his promise to take up the Crusader's mantle to atone for killing his Archbishop. Addressing the Patriarch and his colleagues, Parliamentary barons claimed that the King wanted to fight the infidel but a combination of technicalities and practicalities prevented him from fulfilling his profoundest desire. They noted that his coronation oath, which bound him to rule an unruly kingdom straddling the English Channel, predated his oath to rescue Jerusalem. The barons also said it was their legal "opinion" that it was more important for the King's "soul" to defend his kingdom against the "barbrous [*sic*] French" rather than defend Jerusalem against the barbarous Saracens. The King's age, fifty-four, which made him an old man for the time, also ruled out the rigors of a major military expedition in a faraway land. However, the supplicants from Jerusalem did not go away empty-handed. Henry and his barons offered to raise 50,000 marks to hire mercenaries. He would also "recommend" that his younger subjects, including churchmen, take the cross. According to the chronicler Abbot Joan Bromton, Henry himself made the cash offer to the Patriarch, who was described by the chronicler as "discontented" with the King's proposal. The Patriarch complained, "We seek a man, not money. Well near every Christian region sends us money, but no land sends us a prince. Therefore we ask for a prince that needs money, and not money that needs a prince."

Heraclius stormed out of Parliament and set out for Palestine. Henry followed him all the way to the coast, apologizing and offering more excuses. For example, Henry explained, his sons would rebel against him once he left the country as they had done in the past. The Patriarch refused to be mollified and flung the King's previous crime in his face. At one point, the histrionic prelate bared his neck to the King and said, "Do by me as thou didest by that blessed man Thomas of Canterbury, for I would prefer to be slain by thee than by the Saracens, for thou art worse than any Saracen."

The Patriarch crossed the channel, with the King still in tow, still apologizing, but still unwilling to commit to the foreign adventure. In Normandy in May 1185, Heraclius met with Henry and the King of France, demanding that at least one of them return to the Holy Land with him. Both monarchs refused. Less than a century old, the chivalrous idealism of liberating the birthplace of Jesus had become passé. When the Patriarch returned to Jerusalem empty-handed, chroniclers reported that hysteria overwhelmed the Christian inhabitants.

The panic-struck Jerusalem Heraclius returned to was controlled by the Templars, who dominated the king and at times served as kingmakers. Baldwin IV died soon after Heraclius' return, and his infant nephew, Baldwin V, was proclaimed king at a time when the desperate nation needed strong leadership. The Templars stepped in to fill the power vacuum. The infant king died only seven months after his coronation at the order's headquarters, the Temple of Solomon. The Grand Master, Gerard de Ridefort, picked the new rulers: Sibylla, the mother of the deceased infant, and her second husband, Guy de Lusignan. To enforce the succession, the Templars surrounded the royal palace with troops and sealed the gates of the city to keep out rival claimants to the throne. De Ridefort had in his possession the royal crown and other regalia, which he gave to the Patriarch with orders to crown Sibylla and Guy at the Church of the Resurrection. Emphasizing their authority, the Templars hosted the post-coronation feast at their Temple of Solomon.

De Ridefort's king-making was condemned and caused dissension among the barons at a time when the Christians needed to present a united front to the barbarians who were literally at the gates. Guy de Lusignan was renowned for two things: his physical beauty and his corrupt nature. His reputation was so bad that his own brother, Geoffrey de Lusignan, declared, "Since they have made *him* a King, surely they should have made *me* a God!" Worse, the powerful Count Raymond of Tripoli, enraged that he had not been offered the crown, deserted the city, taking his much-needed troops with him. Many other nobles also refused to pay homage to de Ridefort's nominee.

While the Templars and the secular knights engaged in ruinous power politics, Saladin spent his time preparing for the assault on the Christian capital.

In May 1187, Malek-el-Afdal, Saladin's son, crossed the Jordan and invaded Palestine at the head of 7,000 men. De Ridefort sent messengers to all the Templar fortresses in the area for reinforcements, but he was able to muster a pitiful 130 knights to oppose 7,000 invaders. With their typical suicidal bravery, the tiny force of Templars and a handful of Hospitallers attacked the Saracens at the River Kishon. In the ensuing massacre, all the Hospitallers and Templars were slaughtered or captured except for De Ridefort and two of his men, who managed to break free.

Uninterested in ransom, the victors cut off the heads of the knights, including the Hospitaller's Grand

Master, and impaled them on their lances. The grisly procession then marched on to Hattin, the only fortress that stood between their army and the capital.

On July 4, 1187, Saladin, with 80,000 cavalry and infantry, met the Christian forces at Hattin near Jerusalem. As usual, the Templars placed themselves in the forefront of the army. They attacked and Saladin's men fell back under the sheer fury of the assault. An Arab chronicler and eyewitness overcame the prejudice typical of medieval historians and praised the courage of the enemy. "Never have I seen a bolder or more powerful army, nor one more to be feared by the believers in the true faith," the chronicler, a doctor of law, wrote.

Saladin set fire to the dry grass that separated the two armies, and an ill wind blew the smoke toward the Christian knights, blinding them. Another chronicler, Abbot Radulph of Coggleshale, reported that morale among the Christians was already poor because of the "cowardly behavior" of the Patriarch Heraclius. According to custom, the Patriarch was supposed to march in front of the army, bearing the True Cross. After failing to secure the aid of European powers, Heraclius failed to show up for the crucial battle and left the suicidal task of leading the army to the Bishops of Ptolemais and Lydda.

The most serious charge against the Templars alleged that their incompetence caused the defeat at Hattin, which led to the fall of Jerusalem. According to the anti-Templar party, Gerard de Ridefort insisted on attacking Saladin's forces, despite the overwhelming superiority of the enemy. The Crusaders' secular leader, Guy of Tripoli, wanted to fall back on Jerusalem. De Ridefort publicly accused Guy of cowardice, and the humiliated nobleman felt compelled by honor to give the suicidal order to attack. The entire Christian army was destroyed in the battle. Although some chroniclers blamed the Templars' reckless insistence on the doomed assault, other historians placed the blame on Guy of Tripoli, who fled the field before the outcome of the battle had been decided, abandoning the Templars and Hospitallers.

Guy's desertion was a catastrophe for the Christian forces. One of the luckless standard-bearers, the Bishop of Ptolemais, was killed, and the Bishop of Lydda was taken prisoner. Worst of all in an age of profound superstition, the True Cross fell into the hands of the infidel. The King of Jerusalem and the Templars' Grand Master were also captured. The Hospitallers' Grand Master managed to escape and reached the city of Ascalon, but died of his wounds a day later. Saladin's secretary, Omad'eddin, underlined the powerful hold of superstition when he wrote, "The capture of this cross was more grievous to them than the captivity of their King."

The Templars were admired for their bravery and even Saladin's secretary felt pity for the humiliation these once great warriors experienced after capture. The scribe's vivid imagery remains powerful centuries after the debacle. "I saw thirty or forty tied together by one cord. I saw in one place, guarded by one Mussulman, two hundred of these famous warriors, gifted with amazing strength, who had but just now walked forth amongst the mighty; their proud bearing was gone; they stood naked with downcast eyes."

The number of prisoners taken was so immense, the victors ran out of cord and had to use the ropes that held up their tents. After the captives had been secured, Saladin summoned the most prominent of them to his tent: King Guy of Jerusalem, the Grand Master De Ridefort, and a French baron, Reginald de Chatillon. The baron had become infamous in the Holy Land for attacking unarmed Muslim pilgrims en route to Mecca. The devout Saladin loathed the sacrilege committed by de Chatillon. At first, he played the gracious host with his captives. In keeping with the Muslim custom of hospitality, the sultan offered the King and de Ridefort a refreshing bowl of sherbet, a rare delicacy in that climate. When de Chatillon tried to sample the refreshment, Saladin stopped him and ordered the nobleman to proclaim his belief in Mohammed, whom he had profaned by attacking pilgrims en route to the prophet's birthplace, or face immediate execution. De Chatillon refused to renounce his faith, and Saladin slashed the knight's shoulder with his scimitar. The blow was not fatal, and the sultan's bodyguards finished the job by hacking the Frenchman to pieces.

Two days after this royal reception, Saladin dealt with the rest of the captives. He assembled his entire army to witness their fate. As a trumpet sounded, all the Templars and Hospitallers were brought before the sultan. The knights were given the same offer de Chatillon had refused. If they renounced Christ, embraced Islam, and accepted Mohammed as their prophet (and submitted to a painful circumcision), their lives would be spared. An Arab chronicler reported that every single knight refused and was decapitated on the spot while Saladin "sat with a smiling countenance." Some of the executioners displayed such dexterity with their swords that the audience broke out into spontaneous applause. Saladin's secretary, Omad'eddin, who had once praised the Christians' valor, described their slaughter with equal enthusiasm. "Oh, how beautiful an ornament is the blood of the infidels sprinkled over the followers of the faith and the true religion!" Two hundred and thirty Templars, the Master of the Temple in London later wrote, were left to rot where they were slain for three days. Christian hagiographers claimed that "celestial rays of light played around the corpses of those holy martyrs."

De Ridefort also rejected Saladin's offer of conversion or death, but the Grand Master was spared because it was presumed that the Templars in Europe, whose wealth was by now legendary, would raise a huge ransom.

With the annihilation of the Christian army, the Saracens overran some forty cities and castles in the Holy Land, including many Templar strongholds.

By September 20, 1187, Saladin's army had reached the walls of Jerusalem. Inside, only two Templars remained in the Temple of Solomon. But the leaderless city managed to hold out for fourteen days before the invaders breached the walls. As a last act of desperation and faith, Queen Sibylla, her ladies in waiting, noblemen, and priests marched barefoot to the Holy Sepulchre to pray for their deliverance. The queen and her courtiers did penance by cutting off their hair and standing in tubs of cold water on the same site where Christ suffered, Mount Calvary. But it was too late for prayer. The Muslim banner already flew from the city's ramparts.

A Syrian-French chronicler blamed the victims for their fate. "Our Lord Jesus Christ would not listen to any prayer that they made; for the filth, the luxury and the adultery which prevailed in the city did not suffer prayer or supplication to ascend before God."

Despite their physical absence, the Templars continued to play a mystical role in the tragedy that ensued. On October 2, 1187, the Saracens entered the city and went straight to the Temple of Solomon. Their haste was fueled by religious fervor. The Temple site was sacred to Muslims as the place where the Prophet Mohammed ascended into heaven. Islam considered the Templars' appropriation of the building an act of desecration. Muslim priests (*imams*) and scholars crowded into the Temple and shouted "*Allah akbar!*" ("God is victorious!") After ejecting the Christians who had had the temerity to remain there, Saladin entered the Temple and reconsecrated it to Allah.

The Templars had erected a huge building next to the Temple as a residence and granary, which obscured much of the sacred site from view. The Muslim conquerors tore down the structure and the new space was carpeted to serve as a place of prayer. The last vestige of the Templar presence in Jerusalem had been eliminated.

The Christians paid a ruinous ransom to free the King of Jerusalem and the Grand Master of the Temple.

Instead of gold, entire cities were turned over to the conquerors in return for the captives' freedom. Eleven strategic cities and fortresses vital to the defense of the Holy
Land, including Ascalon, Gaza, Jaffa, and Nablus, were
surrendered. In 1188, the recently liberated Gerard de
Ridefort turned up in Antioch, where the surviving
Templars had regrouped after the fall of the capital.

The loss of Jerusalem and the desecration of the
Holy Places traumatized the apathetic West and galvanized the armies of Europe to action. Soon after news of
the calamity reached Western Europe, a contingent of
300 knights and a small armada set sail from Sicily.
Abandoning their comfortable life in Europe, every able-
bodied Templar, admiring chroniclers reported, left their
monasteries and rushed to the Mediterranean, where
they embarked for Palestine from the ports of Genoa,
Pisa, and Venice. The slippery King Henry II of England
declined to make the trip, but he soothed his conscience
by making a huge cash donation to pay for the defense of
the besieged city of Tyre in Palestine. The trusted
Templars were assigned the task of delivering the money,
but when they arrived at the port of Tyre, they found
that the defenders had already driven away the Muslim
besiegers. Conrad of Montferrat, the military ruler of
Tyre, demanded Henry's money as a reward for his
success. The Templars immersed themselves in local

politics and refused to hand over the cash because Conrad was engaged in a bitter contest for the throne of Jerusalem with Guy de Lusignan, the Templars' candidate for King. Conrad wrote both King Henry and the Archbishop of Canterbury furious letters condemning the Templars' intransigence, which added to their growing disrepute in Europe.

Saladin may have regretted his greed and wished he had killed the Templars' Grand Master when he slaughtered the rest of the order. Within a year of his release, Gerard de Ridefort led a contingent of Templars and reinforcements from Europe out of their stronghold at Tyre and marched on Acre, where they laid siege to the pivotal fortress, which was the major port of entry for pilgrims from Europe. Saladin rushed to Acre to raise the siege. On October 4, 1189, the Christian army attacked Saladin's camp. Instead of leading the charge, the Templars held back, and their strategy saved the day. The Christian attackers enjoyed initial success, once again reaching Saladin's tent, which this time was unoccupied by its famous tenant.

Saladin rallied his forces and the inexperienced Crusaders from Europe panicked and retreated. The wisdom of the Templar strategy now showed itself. As the exhausted Crusaders found themselves squeezed between Saladin's army and the walls of Acre, the fresh band of Templars who had held back entered the battle and stopped the retreat. The Grand Master placed himself in the front line, but he paid for his bravery with his life when an arrow pierced his helmet. The seneschal (the chief financial officer) of the order was also killed, along with more than half the Templar contingent.

The siege of Acre lasted an entire year and nine battles were fought before the Saracens took the city. Historians of the day claimed that 100,000 Crusaders died during the siege, a gross overestimation.

Despite their enormous losses, the Crusaders' ranks were replenished with arrivals from the West. The new recruits were the results of the Third Crusade, organized by the Templars' gadfly, William, the Archbishop of Tyre, who turned up at the courts of France and England, where he made effective speeches dramatizing the sacrileges committed by the Muslim enemy and the valorous deeds of the Crusaders desperate for reinforcements from their native lands. William had better luck in England than his predecessors had. The malingering King Henry had died, and his son and successor, Richard the Lion-Hearted, unlike his father, loved a good fight. The long dormant chivalric ideal of the Crusade revived in Europe under William's oratory, and a new generation of kings and nobles was inspired to take the cross. Richard and his long-time nemesis (and reputed one-time lover), Philip Augustus of France, put aside their trans-Channel tug-of-war over French territory to wage holy war on the infidel.

In May 1191, the new allies sailed into the Bay of Acre. By now, the Templars had turned into a virtual brand name. Lay membership in their order became so fashionable that many secular knights placed themselves under the command of the new Grand Master, an Englishman named Robert de Sablé, and wore with pride the Templar's red cross and white mantle over their armor.

The order's most enthusiastic publicist, the dispossessed Bishop of Acre, James of Vitry, described the penchant they enjoyed among the cream of European royalty and nobility. "The name of their reputation and the fame of their sanctity," wrote the Bishop, perhaps overexcited by the prospect of regaining his Bishopric, "like a chamber of perfume sending forth a sweet odour, was diffused throughout the entire world, and all the congregations of the saints will recount their battles and glorious triumph over the enemies of Christ. Knights from all parts of the earth, dukes and princes, after their example, casting off the shackles of the world, and renouncing the pomp and vanities of this life and all the lusts of the flesh for Christ's sake, hastened to join them, and to participate in their holy profession and religion."

The fresh infusion of Anglo-French forces tipped the balance of power, and within six weeks of Richard and Philip's landing at Acre, the army of Saladin fled, leaving the city undefended and open to the Christian victors.

Before they took possession of the prize, the Templars demonstrated their talent as diplomats and supervised an orderly division of the spoils among the fractious allies. Richard, Philip, their major vassals, and renegade Turkish emirs who had allied themselves with the Christians met in the tent of the Grand Master, where they signed a treaty to avoid disastrous squabbles over control of the city. The Templars' role as referee was pivotal among the hotheaded conquerors, who brought their European feuds with them to the Holy Land. The Templars prevented civil war from breaking out when the choleric Richard tore down the banner of the Duke of Austria and threw it into a ditch. Templar knights physically placed themselves between the outraged Germans and Richard's men and defused the situation. Richard was so enamored of the Templars that he took up residence in their new Temple in Acre. The Temple provided a physical buffer between Richard and his dubious ally, Philip of France, who chose to reside in the fortified center of the city.

The energetic Richard had been busy during his trip from England to the Middle East, picking up valuable real estate along the way. Sailing from the Sicilian port of Messina en route to Palestine, Richard made a brief detour to Cyprus to settle an old score with the island's ruler, Isaac Comnenus, who had insulted Richard's bride Berengaria and his sister when the women's' ship was blown off course and sought refuge in a Cypriot port. Richard disembarked his entire force at Cyprus, stormed the port city of Limissol and gained control of the entire island. The King lost no time converting his conquest into cash by selling the island to the Templars, who paid him 300,000 *livres d'or* in cash, an indication of their immense wealth and another reason Richard loved these well-heeled monks.

Holding Acre as an important beachhead, Richard and his allies felt free to begin the reconquest of the interior of the Holy Land.

From Acre, Richard's army began to move south along the coastline to the strategic citadel of Ascalon. Breaking with tradition, the Templars placed themselves in the rear of the Crusader forces for some unexplained reason. Saladin resisted the Crusaders at every point along the way. When the Christian army passed Jaffa, midway between Acre and Ascalon, Saladin attacked, and the battle lasted eleven days. But the Muslim leader was unable to stop the Christian tide, and the march on Ascalon continued.

The Templars were industrious during the campaign and took the opportunity to enrich themselves by moonlighting. After each day's fighting, while the rest of the troops rested, a contingent of Templars and their Turkish allies launched cattle raids, which began at midnight. They plundered the countryside and returned to camp at dawn loaded down with oxen, sheep, and anything else of value they could carry or herd. Then, after little rest, they would join the main force for the new day's struggle.

On one midnight foray, the Templars' acquisitiveness almost led to their annihilation when they found themselves surrounded by 4,000 mounted Muslims. Just as they were about to be cut to pieces by the overwhelming force of the enemy, King Richard, accompanied by the Earl of Leicester and his men, appeared and rescued the Templars.

On the great plain outside Ramleh, halfway between Jaffa and Ascalon, Saladin made one last attempt to halt the Crusaders' advance. Wave after wave of his Bedouin cavalry and infantry, which Richard's companion, the Christian chronicler Geoffrey de Vinisauf, described as stretching "from the sea-shore to the mountains," hurled themselves against the Christian ranks, but failed to break through. Geoffrey de Vinisauf claimed it was Richard's presence at the very forefront of his army that held the line against the Muslim attack. Saladin and his army fled the field and barricaded themselves inside the fortress of Ramleh, which was the only obstacle between the Crusaders and the ultimate prize, Jerusalem.

Richard for a moment turned his attention away from Saladin and marched on Gaza, which had symbolic significance for the Templars since it had been their main fortress and had been occupied by the Saracens after the debacle at Hattin four years earlier. After capturing the city, Richard returned it to the Templars. With Saladin's army bottled up in Ramleh, Ascalon soon fell, and the Crusaders now controlled the entire coastline of Palestine only six months after their arrival in Acre.

Saladin did not trust the sturdiness of the walls of Ramleh and abandoned the city for the better-fortified Jerusalem. Winter arrived and with it torrential rains that made travel impossible. The Templars wintered in Gaza, while Richard stayed in Ascalon, whose crumbling walls he rebuilt during the break in fighting.

After the rains subsided, the Christian army advanced to within a few miles of Jerusalem. Then, within sight of the prize, the Christian coalition fell apart. Quarrels among the French, German, and English forces almost turned into open warfare.

Saladin took advantage of the Crusaders' disarray and laid siege to Jaffa. This shocked the Christians back into unity. The Templars marched on Jaffa, while Richard reached the city by sailing up the coast. The combined Christian forces beat back Saladin's army, and Jaffa remained in Christian hands.

The Templars had played a pivotal role throughout the Third Crusade, and they now attempted to play a similar role in ending it—with mixed results. Realizing that the internecine squabbling of the Crusaders might lead to a calamitous defeat by Saladin, as evidenced by the near loss of Jaffa, the Templars called a council of the leaders of the European armies. They advised Richard to abandon his attempt to recapture Jerusalem and sign a three-year truce with Saladin. The Christians would retain control of the coastal cities, with the exception of the fortress of Ascalon, which would be demolished. Best of all, Saladin agreed to give Christian pilgrims free access to the Holy Places in the capital. The First Crusade was launched when such access had been denied, and the Templar treaty could be considered a success since it reopened the city to pilgrims. But European chroniclers condemned the order for dissuading the Crusaders from retaking the city.

Richard's close relationship with the Templars did not end with the Crusade. During his stay in Palestine, the King had managed to irritate so many of his nominal allies, especially the Duke of Austria, Richard felt he had to return to Europe in disguise. Consulting with his confidant, Robert de Sablé, the Grand Master of the Temple, they agreed that the King and his Queen should travel separately. With much fanfare to draw attention away from her husband's departure, Queen Berengaria made the return trip by ship, sailing through the Straits of Gibraltar to England. Richard kept his itinerary a secret and traveled by land and sea. He planned to dock at an Adriatic port, then continue his journey on horseback. The Templars had an entire fleet at their disposal, and they loaned Richard one of their ships for the trip home. The King disguised himself as a Templar and traveled with four members of the order, embarking from Acre on October 15, 1192. His ruse failed, and he was recognized and seized while passing through Vienna by Duke Leopold of Austria, who still held a grudge against Richard for tearing down his banner in the Holy Land. Richard spent two years in captivity before a huge ransom raised in England gained his release. Back in England, he demonstrated his gratitude toward the Templars by granting them the manor of Calow.

In 1195, Robert de Sablé was replaced as Grand Master by Gilbert Horal, who set out for Palestine from

GOD'S BANKERS: The ruins of the Chapel of Our Lady of the Temple in Lanieff, France. Besides their headquarters in Palestine, the Knights Templars held monasteries, castles, and churches throughout Europe which also served as banks where royalty and aristocrats could deposit their wealth at one location and withdraw it from another, the prototype of today's branch banking. (*Marc Garanger*)

France, where he had been grand preceptor of the order. Horal lost no time once he arrived in the Holy Land and went on a building binge, erecting a series of fortresses, whose impressive ruins continue to remind us how important a role the Templars played in defending the Christian territory. The most important fortress erected by Horal was the Pilgrim's Castle, which protected the road from Acre to Jerusalem. The citadel was a marvel of its day, and its ruins remain a tourist attraction to this day. Two ten-story towers loomed over the castle. The thick walls, fifteen feet thick and forty feet high, enclosed a large, self-sufficient city, which included a lavish palace for the Grand Master, a Gothic church, vineyards, gardens, orchards, fishponds, and pasture lands for animals to provide meat during sieges. The castle's most important feature for withstanding sieges was a fresh water spring inside the walls.

Despite widespread condemnation for failing to retake Jerusalem, the Templars' decision to make peace with the Saracens allowed Christian Palestine to survive for another century. The Victorian historian, Charles Addison, insisted, "The Latin Kingdom of Palestine was preserved and maintained solely by the exertions of the Templars and the Hospitallers. No action of importance was ever fought with the infidels in which the Templars did not take an active and distinguished part."

While they continued to defend the Holy Land, the Templars' operations in Europe expanded as they performed an impressive variety of tasks—hosting kings, serving as their bankers, mediating for the Pope, and acting as bill collectors.

Richard's brother and successor, King John, enjoyed an even closer relationship with the order than his sibling had. John used the London Temple as a royal residence, staying there for weeks at a time and conducting business within its walls. The signature of Amalric de St. Maur, Master of the Temple of London, appears on a deed executed by King John in 1203, granting a dowry to his wife. The Templars were so trusted that John deposited his entire fortune at the Temple in London. King Philip Augustus of France stored vast amounts of gold and silver in the order's Paris branch. After being excommunicated by the Pope, who also placed his country under interdict, King John was persuaded to submit to the papacy's demands by two Templars who had been delegated the task by the papal legate in England, Pandulph. King Richard's widow, Berengaria, deposited her dowry in the London Temple and asked the Templars to persuade her brother-in-law to repay a loan she had made him of several thousand pounds, a fortune in those days.

The Templars found themselves participating in history as it happened when King John was forced to sign the Magna Carta by rebellious nobles after defeating him in battle. John fled to the protection of the Templars in London, where the victorious barons visited him and dictated their demands. John was even more generous than his brother toward the order. He granted the Templars the entire island of Lundy and huge tracts of land at Radenach and Harewood in the county of Hereford.

While the Templars' power and influence in Europe grew, their fortunes in Palestine swung back and forth between great triumphs and near annihilation. But as their voluminous correspondence with various Popes and other important figures in the West indicates, the Templars kept busy with grand plans for conquest.

In a letter to Pope Honorius in 1217, the Grand Master in Palestine, William de Chartres, boasted of the successes of the order, but the imploring nature of the message undercut his bravado. De Chartres wrote that the Templars had so intimidated Saphadin, the Sultan of Egypt, that the ruler feared leaving the safety of his capital. Despite their military achievements, the Templars were overwhelmed by a huge influx of pilgrims from Europe, among them a royal flush of visitors including the King of Hungary and the Dukes of Austria and Moravia, and their guests had exhausted the Templars' resources, in particular food and horses.

Compounding the problem, the harvest in Palestine had failed and the Christians were facing famine. William de Chartres begged the Pope to send grain, which had been promised but had failed to arrive. The Templars' cavalry, its most effective component, suffered a severe shortage of horses, and the Grand Master asked the Pope to send replacements to put his knights back in the saddle.

De Chartres' letter may have exaggerated the desperation of the order, since it had enough resources to launch a major attack a year later on the Egyptian stronghold of Damietta, after which the ambitious Templar leader planned to march on Jerusalem.

In May 1218, a Templar armada sailed out of Acre and landed at the mouth of the Nile. Joined by secular Crusaders who had traveled overland, they proceeded on to Damietta, where they began a year-long siege. De Chartres did not live to see the outcome of the campaign. Soon after his arrival in Egypt, plague broke out, and he became one of its many victims. Peter de Montaigu, the Grand Preceptor of Spain, hurried from Europe to take his place.

The chronicler James of Vitry, Bishop of Acre, sent reports of the Templars' exploits back to Europe, which promoted their legendary status there. Vitry described epic sea battles on the Nile, including one in which a huge Templar galley sank, killing every member aboard. But even a setback like that reinforced the warriors' reputation as martyrs for the faith.

The Templars and their allies were more successful on land. After withstanding the siege of Damietta for a year, the city's inhabitants launched a cavalry attack on the Crusaders' camp. The Christian troops panicked, and the entire army was in danger of annihilation, but the Templars stood their ground and repelled the Egyptian charge. The secular Christians regrouped and together with the Templars destroyed the Egyptian army. Undefended, the city of Damietta fell to the Crusaders.

The Christian forces did not get to savor their victory for long. Taking advantage of their absence in Palestine, the Sultan of Damascus invaded from the north, captured Caesarea, and laid siege to the Templars' principal stronghold, the Pilgrim's Castle.

Despite their great wealth in Europe, the Templars in the Holy Land seemed perpetually broke. In a letter to the Bishop of Ely in England, the Grand Master Peter de Montaigu boasted about the successful campaign against Damietta and vividly described a series of sea battles between the Templar and Egyptian fleets along the coast of Palestine. But the last paragraph of the Grand Master's letter revealed his real reason for writing. De Montaigu predicted, "If we are disappointed of the succour we expect in the ensuing summer, all our newly acquired conquests, as well as the places that we have held for ages past, will be left in a very doubtful condition. We ourselves ... are so impoverished by the heavy expenses we have incurred in prosecuting the affairs of Jesus Christ, that we shall be unable to contribute the necessary funds, unless we speedily receive succour and subsidies from the faithful." The modern reader is left to wonder why the Grand Master didn't solicit funds from his own treasure houses in Europe, since the Western branches of the order made loans to so many other applicants throughout its history. The order may have remained so rich in the West because it failed to finance its members in the East.

After initial successes due to the absence of the Crusader armies, which were occupied in Egypt, the Sultan of Damascus' campaign in Palestine failed. His forces were driven from the walls of Pilgrim's Castle and back across the border into Syria.

Emboldened by their victories in Damietta and the defeat of the Sultan of Damascus, the secular leaders of Palestine became greedy and overreached their primary goal, securing the Holy Land against Muslim encroachment. Ignoring the Grand Master's advice, restless Crusaders from Europe pressured him to join them in an attack on the Egyptian capital of Cairo. Seizing cities outside of Palestine for plunder was not what the Crusaders had been sent from Europe to accomplish, the Templar leader reminded them to no avail.

Accompanied by the papal legate, which gave the campaign the tacit approval of the Pope, the army crossed into Egypt and made camp on the River Taphenos, a tributary of the Nile, in October 1222. On the other side of the river stood the immense army of the Egyptian Sultan. The Crusaders' offensive was ill timed, since it occurred during the annual flooding of the Nile. After a dry canal filled up with rainwater, the Sultan sent his galleys across it and on to the Nile, where the fleet now faced the Crusaders' southern flanks camped on the banks of the river. Rushing down from Syria, the Sultan of Damascus got his revenge by blocking the Crusaders' northern route. Hemmed in on both sides, the Christian army suffered a further calamity when the Nile overflowed and all the army's provisions were swept into the sea. As the waters continued to rise, the army also lost its horses, carriages, and military equipment. In a desolate letter to the Templars' Preceptor of England, which contrasts with his previous boastful dispatch to the Bishop of Ely, the Grand Master wrote a succinct description of the disaster: "We lost everything we had." Trapped by the overflowing Nile and two Muslim armies, de Montaigu lamented, "We were without food, and being caught and pent up like fish in a net, there was nothing left for us but to treat with the sultan."

"Treat" was a face-saving euphemism for surrender. The Grand Master ransomed his army by returning the great prize of Damietta and handing over hostages. He eagerly accepted an eight-year truce. As a *douceur*, the Egyptian sultan threw in some nuggets, such as the return of the True Cross and Christian prisoners captured during the campaign against Cairo. The surrender of their city enraged the Christian inhabitants of Damietta, especially its new bishop, James of Vitry, who had been the Templars' biggest booster. The Bishop and his chancellor wanted to defend the city, but the Grand Master refused after inspecting the city's weakened walls. As he explained in a letter to the Temple in London, the Templars had run out of money and men. Vitry's vitriol was understandable, since he was one of the hostages handed over to secure the truce. Reflecting the chivalric niceties that both sides displayed during the grim history of the Crusades, the Grand Master mentioned in his letter to England that the Sultan honored the truce and fed the starving Christian soldiers from his own granary.

Despite the calamity in the Holy Land, back in Europe, the Templars continued to prosper and their services were sought by many crowned heads. Warriors, architects, diplomats—these medieval "Renaissance" men wore many hats.

In 1223, a year after the debacle on the Nile, the Templars got into a rare spat with their frequent employer, Henry III of England. The dispute grew so venomous that the King sought the Pope's intervention. The papal bull of 1223, "De Insolentia Templariorum Reprimenda," sided with Henry and listed his complaints against the order, which included their refusal to pay taxes and their cronyism with Templar-appointed judges who displayed bias in lawsuits between royal tax collectors and the order. The bull appointed two English abbots to prepare further charges against the Templars. The investigation went nowhere. It seems that the Templars were too good at the jobs they performed for their royal patron for him to pursue his complaints against them. A year after the bull's promulgation, Henry asked the English head of the Templars, Alan Marcell, to negotiate a truce with the King of France. Relations between the King and his former tax evaders had become so warm that Henry took up residence at the Temple in London at this time. The following year, Henry called on Marcell's diplomatic skills again, sending him to Germany to arrange the King's marriage to the daughter of the Duke of Austria.

The Templars were even better bankers than diplomats, and their financial savvy gained them great wealth. Despite personal vows of poverty, the Templars were financial innovators and introduced branch banking to medieval Europe. Bankrolled by bequests from the dead who hoped to bribe their way into heaven, the Templars lent vast sums of money to out-of-pocket monarchs and became bankers for virtually every throne in Europe. Even Muslim rulers enjoyed the services of their nominal enemy and borrowed heavily from these fiscal wizards. The Templars were to the Middle Ages what the Fuggers were to the Renaissance and the Rothschilds were to the nineteenth century.

Henry III did all his banking at the Temple. During his reign, the Royal Treasury was deposited at the Templars' London headquarters. The King repaid a loan to the Count of Flanders in annual installments, drawn from Henry's funds on deposit at the Templars' branch in Flanders. The immense wealth of the order was demonstrated by another payment that Henry made—10,000 marks—to the Byzantine Emperor, using the King's account at the Templar branch in Constantinople.

The Templars were royal favorites on the other side of the English Channel as well. In 1224, Philip II of

DEATH INSURANCE: Wealthy landowners often bequeathed part or all of their real estate and valuables to holy orders like the Templars as "insurance" to finesse their entry into heaven. One such property is shown here: Temple House in Ballymote, County Sligo, Ireland. (*Michael St. Maur Sheil*)

France left the order 100,000 pounds in his will. The King must have felt the need to buy a lot of redemption and salvation with such a generous bequest.

The Templars also became an indispensable part of the "business" of travel to and from the Holy Land. Their innovative branch banking was not reserved for crowned heads. A pilgrim or Crusader was able to deposit money at a Templar monastery/bank in a European city, then redeem these medieval travelers' checks upon arrival in the Holy Land. The Templars became Europe's primary moneychangers. Indeed, the check was invented by the order.

Because the Templars had monasteries throughout Europe and the Middle East, they became the clearing-house for new ideas from Islamic and Judaic culture and introduced innovations from the Islamic world, which was technologically more advanced than the barbarians of Western Europe. The Templars were the first Europeans to use the magnetic compass. They contributed to improvements in surveying, mapmaking, road building, and navigation. As a kingdom within a kingdom, they had their own seaports, shipyards, and fleets, all of which were used for both military and commercial purposes.

The Templars carried on an extensive Atlantic and Mediterranean sea trade, opening up the isolated, insular nations of Europe during the Dark Ages. The Templars' trading extended as far north as England and as far east as the Holy Land. English linen and other goods were transported in Templar ships to the Atlantic port of La Rochelle in France, then in order to avoid the Muslim-controlled Straits of Gibraltar, the exports were carried overland to Mediterranean ports, where they were reloaded on Templar ships and delivered to eager customers in Palestine.

Heeding Clause 53 of their charter, in which St. Bernard decreed, "We direct the attendants of those who are sick, with every attention, and with the most watchful care, diligently and faithfully to administer to them whatever is necessary for their several infirmaries," the Templars operated hospitals throughout Europe and the Middle East. Drawing on the superior knowledge of Arab physicians accumulated during their sojourn in the East, they became adept at the use of drugs and turned out their own physicians and surgeons in the medieval equivalent of medical schools. They promoted the modern principles of hygiene without knowing the microbial basis for their enthusiasm. For two centuries before their fall, the Templars were masters of their medieval universe.

The monks included master stonemasons among their membership. French historian Louis Charpentier claimed that the Templars financed and built the Gothic cathedral of Notre Dame at Chartres in less than thirty years during the thirteenth century.

While the Templars perfected their skills as royal diplomats, financiers, and scientists in Europe, their associates in the Holy Land seemed ossified in their original role as warriors. In 1229, the Templar Preceptor of Antioch, William de Montserrat, decided to enlarge his territory by attacking the fortress of a Muslim neighbor. Like the earlier land grab for Cairo, the Templars' greed led to catastrophe. The defenders swept out of the fortress, and their superior numbers overwhelmed the forces of de Montserrat, who refused to retreat. In the ensuing battle, 100 Templar knights and 300 archers were slaughtered, along with many secular knights and infantry. The victors then marched on Antioch and took the city. In an attempt to put a positive spin on a disastrous campaign, the chronicler Matthew Paris reported that the reckless Montserrat "before he was slain, sent sixteen infidels to hell."

When news of the defeat reached Europe, the Sixth Crusade was launched, financed in large part by the English branch of the order, which contributed a contingent of knights to the leader of the Crusade, the Holy Roman Emperor, Frederick II.

By now, the eight-year truce between Christians and Muslims that followed the surrender of Damietta had expired, and a new war for possession of the Holy Land seemed inevitable with the arrival of the emperor and his troops. Frederick, however, preferred diplomacy to force and sent Templar negotiators to Cairo, where they managed to persuade Sultan al-Kamil to hand over the holy places of Jerusalem, Bethlehem, Lydda, and Nazareth without a fight! The Grand Master of the order at the time, Hermann de Perigord, wrote a euphoric letter to the head of the English Temple, Robert de Sanford, in which he described the Christians' return to the capital after their bloodless victory. "To the joy of angels and of men, Jerusalem is now inhabited by Christians alone, all the Saracens being driven out." The Christian churches and other holy places, which had been converted to mosques, were reconsecrated. "In those spots where the name of the Lord has not been invoked for fifty-six years now, blessed be God, the divine mysteries are daily celebrated. To all the sacred places there is again free access to the faithful in Christ," de Perigord wrote.

The Grand Master's joy was tempered by his complaint that quarrels among the Christian occupants weakened the united face they needed to present to the enemy that still surrounded them. De Perigord lamented that the defense of the kingdom rested largely on the shoulders of the Templars and the few barons who had stayed above the internecine feuds. In the same letter, the Grand Master mentioned that the order was building a new fortress near Jerusalem to protect the capital, but he was pessimistic about the survival of the Christian presence over the long term. "Indeed, we can in no way defend for any great length of time the places that we hold against the Sultan of Egypt, who is a most powerful and talented man, unless Christ and his faithful followers extend to us efficacious support."

The truce of 1229 lasted until 1244, when it was broken by newcomers to the regions, a nomadic tribe known as the Khwarezmian Turks. Fleeing the Mongols from the east, the Turks swept into Palestine and sacked Jerusalem, slaughtering the entire population, including Christians who had sought sanctuary in the Church of the Holy Sepulchre.

The Turks then marched on the Templar stronghold of Gaza. According to the terms of the Damietta truce, the sultans of Egypt and Damascus had promised to fight on the side of the Christians against the Turks, but they deserted their allies and joined the Khwarezmian, despite an ancient blood feud between the two Muslim forces.

In a two-day battle outside Gaza, the Turks wiped out the entire Templar army. Three hundred Templar knights, their squires, and mercenaries hired by the order perished in the conflict. The casualties included the Grand Masters of both the Temple and the Hospitallers. The ferocious Turks did not spare members of the clergy, perhaps because they had participated in the battle as combatants. The warrior Archbishop of Tyre, the Bishop of Saint George, the Abbot of Saint Mary of Jehoshphat, and many other prelates who had taken up the sword against the infidel died by it.

A tiny band of thirty-three Templars and twenty-six Hospitallers managed to escape and fled to the fortress of Ascalon, where they boarded ships bound for the port of Acre, which was better fortified. The Vice-Master of the Temple, who survived the battle of Gaza, wrote in a letter that was read at a general council of the Church assembled by Pope Innocent in Lyon to launch a new Crusade, "There was not a house or a family that had not lost an inmate or a relation." The idealism and fervor of previous Crusades had become passé in Europe, and the response to the Pope's call was a token force of men and money to aid the outmanned Templars.

The Turks pursued the beleaguered survivors and lay siege to Acre in 1246. But the Templar fleet had survived and kept the port of Acre open to reinforcements, which arrived in the form of Templars from the West, who had emptied the order's treasuries to supply the new army.

Within a year, the Templars not only had raised the siege of Acre, but destroyed the once ferocious Turkish army, which was "slain," a chronicler claimed, "to the last man," adding with bloodthirsty enthusiasm that "their very name perished from the face of the earth." The Templars also managed to hold on to several of the many fortresses they had garrisoned for years. Enough of their forces remained in Palestine so that two years later, in 1249, when Louis IX of France arrived, their fleet at Acre was able to join forces with the King and transport the combined armies to Egypt to retake Damietta.

The campaign ended in a huge victory for the Crusaders. The Templars' Grand Master, William de Sonnace, claimed in a letter to the order's Preceptor in England that only one Christian soldier died during the battle for Damietta.

Encouraged by his success, Louis, like many of his predecessors, decided to take the Egyptian capital and put an end to the Muslim threat to Christian Palestine once and for all. The Templars distinguished themselves during the march on Cairo, and the King's friend, the

Lord de Joinville, sent reports back to France praising their exploits. To save energy for the attack on Cairo, Louis ordered his troops to avoid engaging the enemy along the way. However, the Count of Artois, the King's headstrong brother, ignored the order and chased a band of Turks back to their base at the city of Massoura, despite pleas from the Templars not to break ranks. The Turks rallied and counterattacked. The Count paid for his disobedience with his life and those of 300 other warriors, including fourteen Templars.

The Count's demise foreshadowed the fate of the Christian army in the campaign for Cairo. Before conquering the capital, Louis had to take the strategic fortress of Massoura. The King succeeded in capturing the citadel, but the Templar leader, William de Sonnace, died in the battle. Louis was unable to capitalize on his victory. Before they could reach Cairo, the Nile overflowed and drowned thousands of Louis' men. An outbreak of the plague added to the decimation of his ranks.

Exhausted, Louis ordered a retreat to Damietta. His depleted forces were harassed along the way by Egyptian troops. On April 7, 1250, the Saracens captured the King and his entire army.

A huge ransom was paid for the release of the King and major barons. Instead of returning home in shame,

Louis remained in Palestine for four years, restoring crumbling fortresses at Acre, Caesarea, and Jaffa and erecting a new castle at Sidon. Led by the new Grand Master, Reginald de Vichier, the Templars threw themselves into Louis' strategic building projects to strengthen Palestine. The Templars also fought alongside the Lord de Joinville in skirmishes that rid the borders of marauding Bedouins, and together they captured the castle of Panias near the source of the River Jordan.

While the Templars kept the infidels at bay in the Holy Land, they found themselves fighting with their co-religionists back home.

In 1252, Henry III of England resumed his love-hate affair with the Templars and complained that they had become too rich and powerful. Henry found their arrogance insufferable and threatened to confiscate their wealth. Perhaps proving the King's point, the Grand Master dismissed the King's criticism and called him "silly," then added a threat: "So long as thou dost exercise justice, thou wilt reign. But if thou infringe it, thou wilt cease to be King." Centuries before Rousseau formulated *le contrat social* in opposition to the divine right of kings, the Templars threatened to enforce this social contract if the King reneged on his obligations.

Within two years, relations with their royal patron had returned to the more typical congeniality, and the

Temple in Paris put up Henry during a trip to subdue rebellious vassals in his French fief of Gascony. A day after moving into the Temple, Henry ordered a huge banquet to feed the poor. The Templars were expected to pay for the King's largesse, which they did without complaint. Later that day, Henry hosted another feast at the Temple for the King of France. The lavish hospitality of the Templars became so famous that it found its way into contemporary chronicles. Matthew Paris described the wining and dining of the two kings. "Never was there at any period in bygone times so noble and so celebrated an entertainment. [The kings of England and France] feasted in the great hall of the Temple, where hang the shields on every side, as many as they can place along the four walls."

The Templars became four-star hoteliers for kings, prelates, and diplomats throughout Europe. When ambassadors from Castile visited the court of Henry III in England, their royal host put them up at the London Temple, sending over "three pipes" from the royal wine cellar and "ten fat bucks from the royal forest in Essex." He also ordered the mayor and sheriff of London, accompanied by an entourage of civic notables, to pay a courtesy call on the Spanish emissaries at the Temple.

While Henry and the English Templars continued to enjoy a cordial relationship, the King remained unmoved by the plight of their desperate brethren in Palestine. A year after the fete for the King of France, Henry received a series of letters from the order's Grand Master, Thomas Berard, begging for military assistance. Like his grandfather and namesake, Henry II, the King begged off going on Crusade, pleading poverty. There may have been some truth to Henry's excuse, since he was so broke he had to hock the crown jewels in order to send money to the Templars in Palestine. The pawnkeepers for the jewels were the Templars in Paris, where the treasure had been deposited for safekeeping. Historians fail to answer the question which arises at such times of desperation: if the European branch of the order was rich enough to loan the King money to aid the Templars in Palestine, why didn't the European Templars themselves send funds to their colleagues in the East?

Thomas Berard, the Grand Master, did not exaggerate the desperation of the situation in Palestine in his letters to Henry. At the time, a new ruler came to power who turned out to be an even better general than the legendary Saladin. Baybars, the new Sultan of Egypt, had the humblest of beginnings. He was born a Turkish slave, or *Mameluke* (the Arabic word for slave), and rose to the highest office in the land. His military successes earned him the sobriquet the Conqueror, and he lived up to his nickname when he invaded Palestine in 1262 at the head of 30,000 cavalry. Over the next few years of continuous warfare, he routed Templar and Hospitaller armies, which suffered enormous casualties. Both sides committed atrocities of such infamy that descriptions of them turned up in chronicles of the time. But the Christians suffered more. The near extinction of both military orders reverberated all the way back to Europe, where Pope Clement IV mourned the tragedy in an encyclical that lamented, "By the death of so many knights of both orders, the noble college of the Hospitallers and the illustrious chivalry of the Temple are almost destroyed, and I know not how we shall be able, after this, to find gentlemen and persons of quality sufficient to supply the places of such as have perished." The Pope's despair seemed to anticipate Britain's Foreign Minister Sir Edward Grey's elegiac comment on the eve of World War I: "The lamps are going out all over Europe; we shall not see them lit again in our lifetime."

Baybars took one Christian fortress after another. In 1265, he breached the walls of the Hospitaller stronghold of Arsuf, killing ninety members of the order and enslaving another 1,000. The following year, he seized the Templars' Castel Blanco, then marched on their castle at Saphet, which put up a stronger defense and refused to surrender. The Sultan decided to starve the inhabitants into submission by laying siege to the fortress. The siege did not last long. The Templars' Preceptor inside the city ran out of food after a short time and agreed to surrender without a fight in return for a promise of safe passage of 600 Templars to a nearby Christian citadel, which Baybar granted. Unlike his chivalric predecessor, Saladin, Baybar reneged on his promise as soon as he gained control of the city and offered the Templars the typical Muslim Hobson's choice—convert to Islam or die. European chroniclers claimed that, to a man, the Templars resisted conversion and Baybar slaughtered all of them. However, according to the Arab historian and Baybar's biographer, Schafi Ib'n Ali Abbas, two Templars embraced Islam and suffered the painful initiation rite of circumcision. Baybar's apologist excused the slaughter of the remaining Templars, claiming they violated the terms of the promise by refusing to surrender their arms and hiding their valuables.

Baybar continued to live up to his billing as the Conqueror. Within a year of the atrocity at Saphet, he added to his list of conquests the cities of Homs, Belfort, Bagras, the Templar stronghold at Sidon, and the critical ports of Laodices, Gabala, Tripoli, Beirut, and Jaffa. He showed more mercy than he had at Saphet when Antioch fell, killing only seventeen inhabitants and enslaving the rest—100,000 in all.

All of Palestine now lay under Baybars's control, except for the port of Acre, which was about to fall when Edward, the Prince of Wales, son of the malingering Henry III, shamed his father by sailing into the harbor with a fleet that carried a huge army. Baybars's luck ran out, and the new Crusaders pushed the Sultan's troops all the way back to Egypt. The Conqueror agreed to a truce of ten years demanded by the Prince of Wales.

The Prince decided to return to England the way he had left, by ship, mindful of the disastrous land route his great uncle, Richard the Lion-Hearted, had taken into Austrian captivity. Although European feuds made travel on horseback dangerous, sea travel was just as treacherous because of the crude nature of shipbuilding technology at the time, and before leaving Acre the Prince made his will. The trust in which the English royals continued to hold the Templars was attested to by the fact that Thomas Berard, the order's Grand Master, was a witness to the will.

Back in England, the Templars continued their involvement in royal affairs. During Edward's voyage home, his father died. A royal council composed of the Archbishops of Canterbury and York, various bishops, and the entire baronage, rushed in to fill the vacuum of power. They chose the London Temple as the site to declare the absent Edward King and swear allegiance to him. To avert the possibility of civil war during the new King's absence, the council appointed Walter Giffard, the Archbishop of York, and the Earls of Cornwall and Gloucester, as regents. The noblemen used the Temple as their residence, and sent letters from there to the seaborne King via swift galleys, informing him of his father's death and their appointment as viceroys. During the regency, steady streams of edicts were issued from the Temple.

In 1273, a year after Edward's return from the Crusade, the new Grand Master of the Temple, William de Beaujeu, left Palestine and turned up in England for the usual reason—to seek aid for the beleaguered kingdom. But de Beaujeu had another reason for visiting England. During Edward's campaign in Palestine, he had borrowed huge amounts from the Templar treasury. The new King made good on the loan and repaid the Grand Master when he took up residence in the London Temple.

The situation in the Holy Land had become so desperate that the Grand Master of the Hospital there also returned to Europe and made his way to Lyon, France, where the Pope called another council to launch a new Crusade. The two Grand Masters were held in such high esteem that they took precedence over all the

European nobility and ecclesiastics at the assembly. A former resident of Palestine, the Pope vigorously promoted the Crusade and ordered a tax on the clergy to finance the campaign. More important than providing money, the Pope ordered the rulers of Europe to stop quarreling among themselves and take up the cross. Under papal pressure, many kings and princes agreed to go in person to the Holy Land, but they did not have to make good on their promise. During the council at Lyon, the Pope died; without his support, so did the Crusade. Throughout the Middle Ages, enthusiasm for the Crusades waxed and waned. The end of the thirteenth century marked a period of apathy. The nineteenth century historian, Charles Addison, summarized the prevailing mood at the time. "A vast change had come over the spirit of the age; the fiery enthusiasm of the holy war had expended itself, and the Grand Master of the Temple and Hospital returned without succour, in sorrow and disappointment, to the East."

Without arms or money, William de Beaujeu returned to Acre in 1275 and had to rely on diplomacy to accomplish what he could not do by force of arms. The ten-year truce, which had resulted from the Prince of Wales' stunning victories, was about to run out. Like many of his predecessors, the Grand Master was an adept negotiator. Despite a weak hand, he persuaded the Egyptian Sultan, Malek-Mansour, to renew the truce, called the Peace of Tortosa, for another ten years. Both parties agreed to make no encroachments on the other's territories. To avoid future conflicts, the treaty spelled out which cities belonged to the Muslims and which remained in Christian hands.

Despite the elaborate terms of the treaty, the truce did not last long, but after a series of indecisive battles, the exhausted opponents agreed to yet another truce, which also proved short-lived. This time, hostilities were renewed due to an atrocity committed by a group of European mercenaries who had arrived in Acre in search of plunder. They seized nineteen wealthy Egyptian merchants residing in the city, extorted a huge sum from them as ransom, then reneged on the bargain and hanged their captives.

The enraged Sultan of Egypt vowed to exterminate the Christian presence in Palestine and seized the fortress of Margat and the city of Tripoli. Within three years, the Sultan held all of Palestine except Acre and the Templars' headquarters, the Pilgrim's Castle.

In the spring of 1291, the new Sultan, Khalil, decided to deliver the coup de grâce to the Christians by taking their sole link to the outside world, the port of Acre. Enormous for the time, the Sultan's army of 60,000 cavalry and 140,000 infantry assembled outside

HOLY PHILANTHROPY: As their fame in defending the Holy Land grew in Europe, kings and feudal magnates donated not only monasteries but entire cities, including the fortified city shown here, to the Templars, which eventually led to their becoming the wealthiest landowners in Europe. (*Gianni Dagli Orti*)

the city. Engineers began to excavate the ground under the walls to create a breach.

Opposing this ocean of besiegers was a garrison of 12,000 Christian knights and infantry. The defenders knew their only hope lay in the large fleet of Templar and Hospitaller galleys in the harbor, which were ready to take them to safety in Cyprus. The Grand Masters of both orders refused to flee, but noncombatants, mostly women and children, were evacuated to Cyprus. The remaining residents prepared to die defending the city.

The siege lasted six weeks, and the attacks on the walls were incessant. State-of-the-art technology was employed in the assault. The sheer amount of medieval artillery was impressive. More than 600 catapults and battering rams stood outside the walls. One battering ram was so large that 100 wagons were required to move it into place. Higher than the walls and protected by animal hides, mobile towers housed warriors who showered the defenders with arrows and spears. For a while, the Christians managed to set fire to the towers and battering rams and to knock out the engineers and workers trying to undermine the walls. But the fate of the outnumbered defenders was inescapable. Unlike the Crusading ideal, which had sputtered out in Europe, Muslim fanaticism inflamed the entire Middle East, and constant reinforcements arrived to replace the slain attackers.

Thirty-three days into the siege, the siege machines destroyed the city's main tower. The tower had protected the city's double walls, which were now vulnerable to attack. After ten more days, a breach was made in both walls. One of the defenders, the King of Cyprus, panicked when he saw the last obstacle to the invaders removed and fled at night to his ships, which took him and 3,000 of his men back home to Cyprus. The next morning, on May 18, an army of Egyptian Mamelukes attacked the portion of the wall left undefended by the King of Cyprus's desertion and breached it. They made their way to the center of the city, where their advance was halted by mounted knights under the command of the two Grand Masters. Fighting in the narrow streets, the Christians managed to push the Mamelukes back outside the walls.

Unable to repair the breach in the walls, they provided a "living barrier" of steel—themselves—to keep the invaders from reentering the city. The Templars and Hospitallers beat back the army of the Sultan, pausing their efforts only when the Grand Master of the Hospital was critically wounded, and a shower of darts and arrows mortally wounded the Grand Master of the Temple, William de Beaujeu. Templar knights placed their leader on a shield and carried him, still alive, back to the Temple, where he perished. While the fighting continued, de Beaujeu was interred in front of the Temple's main altar.

Some of de Beaujeu's knights panicked at the sight of their fallen leader and fled to the harbor, where ships took them away from the doomed city. Still others fled to the Templar fortress at Sidon and from there sailed to Cyprus and safety.

There remained inside the city only 300 Templars, who fought off wave after wave of Mameluke attackers as they made their way from the walls back to the fortified Temple and shut the gates on the enemy. During this temporary reprieve, they managed to find time to hold a meeting and elect a new Grand Master, the Italian Tibald Gaudin (also called Guadini).

The Temple was a fortress within a fortress and the size of a medium city. It was surrounded by thick walls and towers. The fortress was large enough to hold the palace of the Grand Master, a church, and barracks for knights of lesser ranks. A granary and an enclosure called the Cattle Market allowed the residents to withstand a long siege.

Perhaps aware of the impregnability of the fortress and its provisions, the Sultan and his exhausted army stifled their bloodlust, and the Egyptian ruler offered generous terms of surrender. The Templars would be allowed to evacuate the fortress and make their way unmolested to the harbor, where the Sultan would place his own ships at their disposal. The knights would also be allowed to leave with as much of their treasure as they could carry. The Sultan made a solemn promise to abide by these terms and sent a force of 300 soldiers to escort the evacuees to the port.

The Templars were not the only refugees. A number of women had taken shelter in the fortress, but before they could leave with the knights, some of the Muslim escorts tried to rape the women. The enraged Templars slammed the gates shut, trapping the Muslims and slaughtering all three hundred of them.

The army outside the Temple resumed its attack on the fortress, but the Templars managed to keep the enemy at bay for another day. At that point, the Grand Master realized that continued resistance would only delay the inevitable slaughter. He hoped that if the Sultan knew the reason his escort had been slaughtered, he might agree to another truce. To that end, Gaudin sent the Marshall of the order and several other knights to the Sultan's camp flying a white flag. But the Egyptian ruler had had his fill of diplomacy, and before the emissaries could plead their case, he had them all decapitated. The assault on the Temple resumed.

Unlike his predecessors, the Grand Master Gaudin was not willing to go down with the ship. Instead, he planned to escape on one. Gaudin turned out to be the first Grand Master in the history of the order to abandon his men rather than die fighting with them. With a few companions, Gaudin gathered up the order's portable treasure, including altar ornaments, and sneaked out of a hidden back gate of the Temple. Making his way to the harbor, he boarded a ship that took him and his party to Cyprus.

The handful of remaining Templars was left to their fate, fighting a lost cause, deserted by their leader. The knights retreated to the refuge of last resort, the Temple's massive tower. Wave after wave of Mamelukes hurled themselves at the fortress, but the defenders fought back the attacks and refused to surrender. The Sultan's supply of replacements seemed endless, and an eyewitness account described the tower of corpses that piled up several stories high outside the tower.

The Sultan decided to oust the defenders by undermining the walls of the tower. Engineers propped up the walls with wooden beams while workmen tunneled underneath them. Employing classic siege technique, the invaders waited until the trench was big enough, then set fire to the beams and the walls collapsed. The Templars were spared the indignity of capture and execution as the collapsing tower did the Sultan's work for him, killing all of the defenders.

Although he now controlled the city of Acre, the Sultan made sure that a new wave of Crusaders from Europe would find nothing to recapture. He ordered fires set in four locations and burned the city *almost* to the ground. Today, the ruins of the once great Templar fortress remain a tourist attraction and a sad reminder of the last stand made by the tiny remainder of the Holy Land's last champions.

The Templar presence in Palestine ended with the fall of the fortress. Almost as soon as it fell, the inevitable question arose: Who lost the Holy Land?

A parallel question posed by Saracen chroniclers as well as the Jewish inhabitants of the Holy Land demanded to know, "Where is their God now: where is the God of the Christians?" To cynical minds in search of a scapegoat and an explanation for the failure of a cause that had seemed divine, the blasphemous queries stopped just short of the twentieth century's famous musing, "Is God dead?" The despair implicit in such questions and the fact that they were asked in an Age of Faith underline the crisis Christianity experienced at the turn of the thirteenth century. Crises generate drastic responses, and Europe would take drastic action against the warriors its leaders came to demonize as the men who lost the birthplace of Christ.

This time, the loss of the Holy Land failed to re-ignite the Crusading ideal, and for some reason—perhaps centuries of exhaustion—killed it instead. Cynicism about religion fueled by military failure also generated anticlericalism and antimonasticism, which not only led to the end of the Templars, but also led to the end of the monastic ideal in general and the birth of the Protestant Reformation. Prompted by cynicism rather than idealism, the great movement set in motion by Luther can be interpreted as a final act of religious nihilism rather than a beginning act of reform. It is too simplistic to suggest a simple cause and effect between the embarrassing surrender of a Templar fortress in 1291 and a list of ninety-five grievances tacked to a church door in a German college town 226 years later; yet the connection, however tenuous and indirect, is also unbreakable and inarguable.

The Christian cause in Palestine died under a collapsed trench in 1291, along with centuries of idealism and avarice, and the hopes of altruistic knights and their land-hungry second sons.

PART TWO

Europe

The Templars refused to let the dream of retaking the land of Christ's birth die. After the fall of Acre in the last decade of the thirteenth century, Tibald Gaudin lived in disgrace on Cyprus and died, some said of shame, two years after abandoning his command. Templar leaders gathered in England and elected a new and final Grand Master, Jacques (also known as James) de Molay, who had been Preceptor of the order of the English branch despite his French birth.

Unlike his craven predecessor, de Molay was driven to fulfill the Templars' original brief, the recovery of Palestine. The failure of the Crusading ideal in general, and the misdirected energy of the Templars in particular, were symbolized by the pathetic number of men de Molay was able to recruit for this anticlimactic epilogue to the Crusades. With only 120 followers, de

Molay landed at Acre and was immediately repulsed by the forces of the Egyptian Sultan. De Molay survived and returned to a Europe that no longer idealized the warrior monks in Palestine, but rather resented the wealth and power of the sybaritic ascetics.

The Templars returned to Europe defeated, and to many it seemed unfair that they remained rich. In the divine scheme of things, their wealth appeared to reward failure.

A poem written by Rostan Bergenguier of Marseilles some time between the fall of Acre and the dissolution of the order two decades later asks a series of rhetorical questions that sound more like a prosecutor's brief than verse. Although not lyrical, the poet was prescient in his exhortations about the fate of the order:

> Since many Templars now disport themselves on this side of the sea [i.e. Europe], riding their gray horses or taking their ease in the shade and admiring their own fair locks; since they so often set a bad example to the world; since they are so outrageously proud that one can hardly look them in the face; tell me why the Pope continues to tolerate them; tell me why he permits them to misuse the riches which are offered them for God's service on dishonorable and even criminal ends.

> They waste their money which is intended for
> the recovery of the Holy Sepulchre on cutting a fine
> figure in the world; they deceive people with their
> idle trumpery, and offend God; since they and the
> Hospital have for so long allowed the false Turks to
> retain possession of Jerusalem and Acre; since they
> flee faster than the holy hawk; it is a pity, in my
> view, that we don't rid ourselves of them for good.

While financial success bred envy among the Templars' enemies, it created arrogance and corruption in their own ranks. These flaws increased in proportion to their wealth, power, and complacency. No sin was too insignificant to be attributed to the monks, and they were accused of alcoholism. "To drink like a Templar" was a cliché of the time. They antagonized local church authorities by recruiting excommunicated knights, which robbed the church of its most effective form of punishment and control over disobedient subjects.

While the Templars prospered in Europe, their original raison d'être, protecting the Holy Land, disappeared with the failure of the Crusades. Lacking a mission, they turned their attention and acquisitiveness more and more toward Europe.

In one last military hurrah, at the close of the thirteenth century, the Templars founded another order,

SALVATION FROM DAMNATION: To increase their number, the Templars recruited excommunicated knights, which enraged church leaders because excommunication was a powerful means of controlling wayward warriors who defied the ecclesiastical authorities.

the Teutonic Knights, who set up an autonomous prin-
cipality which overlapped and antagonized Prussia and
Russia for centuries.

During the so-called Crusades of the thirteenth century against the Cathars, members of a heretical sect in
Southern France also known as Albigensians, sought
refuge from persecution in the castles of the Templars,
whose impregnable fortresses prevented the French
from seizing the persecuted group.

The Templars' reputation suffered further when
they engaged in warfare that had no religious justification. In 1298, seven years after losing Palestine, the
Templars allied themselves with their sometime persecutor, Edward I of England, and fought in the battle of
Falkirk against the King of Scotland. Besides damaging
their reputation, the political meddling had disastrous
practical results. Both the Master of the Temple of
London and his second in command, the Preceptor of
Scotland, perished in the battle. During the same
period, Templars injected themselves into a boundary
dispute between the Count of Anjou and his neighbor,
the King of Aragon, and participated in several battles
between the warring magnates.

Despite the Templars' protection of the heretical
Cathars, the papacy remained the order's champion for
a while. The rest of Europe did not share the papal

enthusiasm, and attacks on the Templars by temporal and religious leaders became so pervasive that in 1160 Pope Alexander III issued a series of bulls threatening to excommunicate high-ranking magnates and prelates who had criticized the Templars. In one bull, Alexander reminded his flock of the great services rendered by the Templars in the Holy Land while the rest of Europe ignored the call of the Crusades. In another bull, he ordered the faithful not to pull Templars from their horses! Alexander complained that some bishops had denied the Templars admission to their churches, while others tried to stop them from collecting alms for the poor. Despite their reputation for greed, the Pope praised the order as the most philanthropic foundation in Europe. He condemned clergymen who extorted fees for burying Templars, while others, imitating the custom of kings, turned up at Templar monasteries and demanded to be fed and housed gratis.

Alexander's bullishness about the Templars may have had something to do with the fact that like many secular rulers, he borrowed heavily from them. The Templars served as Alexander's almoners, chamberlains, and keepers of his castles (castellans). As they had done throughout the Holy Land, the Pope set them to building fortresses in the papal lands. A few Templars became Alexander's confidants.

After more than a century of royal and noble deathbed bequests of land and manors, the Templars were the biggest real estate holders in Europe. But by now, rulers resented the pious generosity of their ancestors and wanted to reclaim the largesse of their superstitious forebears.

In contrast to the excellent relations between the Templars and a succession of English Kings, Edward I turned on the men his predecessors had used as bankers, diplomats, and hoteliers. This was the same Edward who, three decades earlier, as Prince of Wales, had fought side by side with the warrior monks in the reconquest of Acre and left his will for safekeeping with them before returning home.

By 1302, the King was broke and owed ruinous back pay to the troops that had helped him pacify Wales. Ignoring the Templars' aid at the battle of Falkirk, the ungrateful monarch seized the treasury of the London Temple, which had been earmarked for their brethren on Cyprus, who were planning another assault on Palestine. The ultimate proto-sophist, Edward justified his expropriation of the order's treasury by arguing that the Templars' wealth had been accumulated for the defense of the Holy Land. Since there was no Christian presence there anymore, Edward decided the order's monies should be distributed to the poor, with the King volunteering to disburse the funds to charity.

The Pope once again rescued the Templars. Under threat of personal excommunication and the interdiction of his kingdom, Edward returned the money, which the Templars sent to Cyprus before the King could change his mind.

Edward did change his mind. Fearing rebellion among his still unpaid troops, he devised another fundraising ruse. With his companion, Sir Robert Waleran, and other followers in full military gear, the King turned up at the Temple in London with an innocent request. He wanted to make sure his mother's jewels, which had been deposited with the monks, were all accounted for. Once the gates of the impregnable fortress were opened to him, Edward and his men ransacked the monastery until they found its cash depository. The King helped himself to 10,000 pounds, an enormous amount for the time, and fled with the loot to the protection of Windsor Castle. This time, the money was not returned.

Edward's greed seemed hereditary. Five years later, upon his son's accession to the throne as Edward II, the new King and his lover, Piers Gaveston, targeted the order's wealth, although the son's avarice surpassed the father's. The new King expropriated 50,000 pounds of silver, along with an unspecified amount of gold and precious stones. The treasure, however, did not belong to the Templars. It had been deposited at the London Temple by the unlucky Bishop of Chester, who trusted the Templars' reputation for honesty but did not realize the order's impotence against royal greed.

By 1306, King Philip IV (the Fair) of France wanted to get rid of the arrogant Templars, but found their army superior in number and equipment to his, and their castles located strategically throughout the kingdom.

The arrogance of the Templars was not the real source of Philip's enmity. The bankrupt, unpopular King had borrowed vast sums of money from "God's bankers" with no hope of repaying them.

Although the Templars later became the source of countless myths and legends, their wealth was real, not fabled. In the early fourteenth century, just before their dissolution, British historian Peter Partner estimates their portable cash wealth—not including lands tied up in perpetuity to titled aristocrats—at 150,000 gold florins, which was equal to half the annual expenses of Edward II and four times the income of one of Edward's rebellious nobles. The French branch of the order's wealth would be a windfall to Philip, whose revenues, unlike those collected by the strong centralized English monarchy, trickled into Paris in maddening drips. More conservative historians than Partner feel the 150,000 florins represented fantasy or wish fulfillment on the part of the desperate King. Whatever the amount, the Parisian Templars' hoard was not hoarded long, but disbursed to their forces in Cyprus in preparation for the campaign against the Saracens.

Philip had more to resent than the wealth of the financial Fifth Column in his capital. He found himself in their debt in another, more embarrassing way. Once, while fleeing a Parisian mob, the King sought refuge in the Templars' citadel in the center of the city. Legend has it that as he cowered inside the fortress, Philip looked around at his luxurious sanctuary and became aware of the wealth of his protectors. Adding to his humiliation was the fact that years earlier, he had tried to join the order as a lay member—and was rejected. The rejection epitomized the arrogance that so irritated Templar critics.

Philip IV was a complex character whom it would be unfair to dismiss as motivated by greed or revenge alone, although both of these emotions did indeed drive him. A classic dilettante and underachiever in youth, the King found religion after the twin disasters of defeat at the battle of Courtrai in 1300 and his wife's death in 1307. Historian Peter Partner represents a minority opinion when he describes Philip as withdrawn and paralyzed by religious self-absorption. The relentlessness with which he pursued the Templars does not suggest the passive-aggressive behavior of a depressed widower or a defeated warrior. Although it led to a gold mine, his persecution of the Templars also reflected genuine concerns about the corruption and sacrilege he believed were being committed at the highest level of monastic society. The fact that the perpetrators happened to be at the top of the financial heap added an irresistible enticement, but did not represent the sole engine of royal will.

The medieval *Weltanschauung* provided an elastic view of who constituted Christ's Vicar, and it was not only the Pope, but also temporal rulers like Philip who ruled by the Divine Right of Kings that wouldn't be questioned until Charles I and Louis XVI lost their heads over the issue centuries later. Although the eradication of the Templars would enrich Philip, he believed he was acting as God's scourge and carrying out His Will in response to Templar sins that, as recent as 100 years ago, were still too salty for historians to report except in the original Latin Vulgate or Middle French.

Philip was a dangerous enemy, whatever the motivation for his enmity. After allegedly murdering two successive Popes, he managed to get one of his cronies, the Archbishop of Bordeaux, elected as Clement V in 1305. The King then demanded that Clement, who was the nominal leader of the Templars, suppress the order. To his surprise, the new Pope temporized to the point of resisting his royal patron, who continued to view Clement as his creature. Clement resented the King's infringement of his autonomy, even though it was largely illusory. The King had forced Clement to abandon Rome and relocate to Avignon, a city-state ruled by a Neapolitan branch of the French dynasty and located just outside France's border. The official reason for this New Rome was that Clement was too ill to make the trip to the old one. The excuse of papal infirmity fooled no one, and the transfer of the Holy See from the Eternal City to a French backwater scandalized the rest of Europe. This period in the history of the papacy came to be known as the "Babylonian Captivity," a disaster of morale equivalent to the Biblical enslavement of the Israelites.

Contemporary chroniclers accused the Pope of other sins besides abandoning Rome, including an affair with a beautiful French countess and the practice of simony—selling religious offices for cash—which was endemic among Clement's predecessors in the papacy and the prelacy. His enemies also claimed that he sold Church relics.

Philip's pressure on the Pope reflected an obsessive desire to wipe out the Templars throughout Europe— even though the wealth expropriated outside the borders of France would not flow into his coffers, but into those of other royals and landed magnates, including dangerous rivals who might put the order's wealth to military use against Philip. As France's autocrat, he did not need papal approval to seize French nationals, even internationally known and respected warriors who were also regarded as holy men. Caesaropapism and Gallicanism, both of which placed royal authority over the rights of the papacy and prelates, provided the theological justification for a land-and-cash grab by the King, but his insistence on shutting down the international conglomerate the Templars had become suggests something more complicated than mere greed or revenge. Perhaps megalomania fueled his pogrom of extermination.

In proclamation after proclamation, Philip decried the moral depravity of the entire order, not just the monastic perverts within his own realm. It was a root and branch argument rather than a call for surgical excision of a few wayward monks who, after centuries of misguided theology and a toxic proximity to the Islamic faith, had gotten their religious practices wrong.

Clement was not able to resist his royal patron for long. Only two months after his coronation, he sent letters to the Grand Masters of the Hospital on the island of Malta and the Temple on Cyprus, commanding them to come to France for the purpose of planning a new Crusade. The Pope's ulterior motives were transparent in his instructions to the Grand Masters: "We order you to come hither without delay, with as much secrecy as possible, and with a *very little retinue*, since you will find on this side of the sea a sufficient number of your knights to attend upon you."

The Grand Master of the Hospital could read between the lines and guessed why the Pope insisted on a minimal bodyguard. The Hospitaller's leader ignored the summons and stayed put in the safety of Malta. His suspicions may have been also aroused by Clement's command to show up with all the order's portable wealth.

The Templar leader, Jacques de Molay, was less cynical and honored the order's original benefactor, the Pope, even though Clement now lived in Avignon and acted more like the Vicar of Philip than Christ. He obeyed all the papal instructions, although he was suspicious enough to bring sixty armed knights along with the Templar treasury when he left Cyprus and appeared in Paris in 1307. De Molay probably thought his money was safe when he deposited it at the Temple in Paris since the monastery-branch bank had safely held so many other depositors' fortunes.

To assuage any suspicions, Philip received de Molay with all the honors accorded a head of state, which, in terms of real estate, the Templar chief was in all but name.

In May of 1308, the King and de Molay traveled together to Poitiers, where the Pope was waiting to discuss a Crusade he had no intention of launching. Philip was in a rush and demanded de Molay confess to various heretical practices. The King strengthened his demand by hinting to Clement through royal intermediaries that if the Pope did not back Philip's charges against the Templars, Clement himself would be proclaimed a heretic. The King's grandiosity in placing himself above the Pope in terms of defining heterodoxy seems less shocking when the location of the threat is kept in mind—in the heart of France surrounded by royal troops. The Babylonian Captivity by definition included a Babylonian Captive.

Clement told Philip flat out that he didn't believe the accusations of heresy against the order, and certainly not the purple practices they were accused of during their initiation rites, which became more baroque and colorful the longer the royal prosecutors took to enlarge their palette. Perhaps the only rule that emerged as true among all the fictitious ones was that there was no Templar rule. The order's detractors told the truth when they maintained that individual members were not allowed to possess a copy of the rulebook and its colorful rites. But the reason had nothing to do with the contents and everything to do with the fact that it did not exist. Despite testimony and innumerable hearings across Europe, no rulebook was ever produced at any Templar trials—with or without the incriminating passages!

As the reality of his weakened position set in, Clement abandoned the Templars and tried to save himself and what was left of papal authority—papal autonomy by now a wistful memory.

During his meeting with de Molay, the Pope made a demand that the usually subservient Grand Master rejected out of hand. Clement wanted the Templars and Hospitallers, centuries-old rivals, to merge into one order. The idea was a papal preoccupation that predated Clement's reign. Philip was also obsessed with a "unite and conquer" strategy that would simplify and solidify his control over one rather than two rich monastic orders.

After the fall of Acre, the public needed a scapegoat, and the Pope at the time, Nicholas IV, was arbitrarily singled out and condemned for failing to send money to the city's defenders when all of Europe had failed to succor the cause. Nicholas counterattacked and claimed that the rivalry between the Temple and Hospital groups had sapped both organizations' energies, and their disunity rather than papal parsimoniousness had caused the fall of the last Christian outpost in the East. Clement borrowed his predecessor's argument in ordering the union of Temple and Hospital.

In two public memoranda propagated in 1306 and 1307, de Molay offered an unconvincing generalization that "innovation is almost always very dangerous," and a specific countercharge with more merit: Nicholas had invented the alleged dissension between Temple and Hospital to cover his own culpability over the loss of Acre. If there was rivalry between the two orders, de Molay maintained, it was a healthy competition that strengthened rather than weakened the orders' military efforts. In fact, ending the friendly antagonism between the orders would aid the infidel and hurt whatever hope the Christian West had of regaining the Christian East. De Molay cited many examples to prove his point: When the Hospitallers enjoyed a spectacular victory, the Templars fought even harder to achieve a similar success. When the Templars sent a showy force of men and munitions to wage a new Crusade, the Hospitallers felt compelled to send an even bigger contingent. It was a game of monastic one-upmanship that benefited the goal of all sides—Christian rule in Palestine. De Molay offered a compelling bit of historical trivia to make his case. Despite both orders' international reputation as belligerent zealots, there was not a single recorded instance of bloodshed between members of the two orders. This religious harmony contrasted with the feuds between secular leaders that had undermined so many wobbly Christian coalitions in Palestine. De Molay also took advantage of the meeting at Poitiers to condemn various European princes, who were robbing the Templars with impunity, reversing a hallowed tradition of giving money to the order instead of stealing from it.

The Grand Master rejected another papal suggestion that might have saved the order as a similar reorganization has preserved their rival, the Hospitallers, to this day.

The Pope urged them to join the forces of the Christian King of Armenia and launch another assault on the Holy Land from the King's base in Asia Minor. De Molay countered that such a tiny force against the tide of Islam would be suicidal and predicted that only a heavily armed combination of knights and infantry, such as the 15,000-strong knights and 5,000 infantry led by St. Louis of France during his temporary success in the Holy Land several decades before, would prevail.

De Molay wasn't being a cynic but a historian when he wrote in a letter to the Pope that such a huge army of the West would more likely be used against the Byzantine emperor in the East, as it had been when Crusaders from Europe conquered Constantinople at the beginning of the previous century.

While de Molay's bureaucratic and Gibbonian arguments against Clement's demands may have been legitimate, his rejection of the Pope's military brief flew in the face of centuries of martial tradition which had once made and would now break the Temple. The vastly different fate of the Hospital remains instructive and tragic in retrospect. During their stay on Cyprus after the fall of Acre, both orders, lacking military purpose, injected themselves into local politics and participated in the military adventures of the island's king. Both organizations possessed fleets that were the envy of Europe. While the Templars' navy remained either in drydock or engaged in trade that had nothing to do with military or religious matters, the Grand Master of the Hospital used his navy to seize the island of Rhodes from the Byzantine emperor in 1309. The Templar base of operation returned to Europe and annihilation, but the Knights of the Order of St. John kept a maritime base far enough away from the intrigues of Europe to preserve it into the second millennium on the island of

Malta, where they fled after the fall of Rhodes to the Ottoman Turks in 1522. One of the big "ifs" of history is if the Templars had had an island of refuge in the Eastern Mediterranean, would they have survived?

While de Molay and Clement squabbled about organizational issues, Philip decided to act on his own. At the same time paid agents of the King spread rumors accusing the Templars of losing the Holy Land and far worse, Philip set about suborning perjury. The King was so desperate to find critics of the order, he resorted to using the most dubious of witnesses. Squin (also Esquin) de Florian, a former resident of the city of Bezieres in Palestine, indicated how low the King had to stoop. Philip himself had imprisoned de Florian for what contemporary chroniclers only described as "iniquities." The King pardoned de Florian, who then swore under oath that the Templars had committed heresy. Another royal witness, Nosso de Florentin, a disgraced Templar who had been sentenced to life in prison by the Grand Preceptor of France for unspecified "impieties," confessed from his dungeon to a series of "abominations" which he and his former brothers had engaged in.

The explicit testimony of the two miscreants must have burned the ears of those who heard the accusations in an era whose barbarity was only surpassed by its prudery.

On the "strength of a condemned criminal's oath," the outraged Victorian Charles Addison sneered, Philip sent bailiffs throughout his kingdom with secret instructions to seize every single member of the order. The instructions included his justification for the seizures. The King pronounced himself shocked—shocked!—at the "atrocities" that he had only recently learned of.

In his letter to the bailiffs, he wrote, "Philip, by the grace of God King of the French, to his beloved and faithful knights . . . A deplorable and most lamentable matter, full of bitterness and grief, a monstrous business, a thing that one can hear without horror, transgressions unheard of, enormities and atrocities contrary to every sentiment of humanity . . . have reached our ears." Even through the filter of a stilted, Victorian-era translation of Philip's letter (Addison's), the modern reader can't help but think Philip's overkill reflected his qualms about the validity of his accusations.

The King's letter contained a laundry list of heinous crimes allegedly committed by the Templars. They were accused of insulting Christ and causing Him more grief than the Romans had, of mocking the crucifix, sacrificing to idols, and engaging in "impure practices and unnatural crimes," which the King daintily failed to elaborate on. The Templars, Philip said, were "ravishing wolves in sheep's clothing."

He offered the accused an escape clause, which was more like a Hobson's choice. The bailiffs were instructed to use torture if necessary to extract confessions, but if the monks voluntarily admitted their crimes, they would be spared death. The King failed to sweeten the offer by specifying an alternative punishment for self-incrimination.

From the start, critics independent of the King criticized the arrests and questioned the legitimacy of the accusations against the Templars and the King's motives in making them. Three weeks after the arrests, a Genoese politician, Cristiano Spinola, complained that cupidity, not piety, prompted Philip's orders. Philip had backed the Pope's demand for a union of Temple and Hospital, and Spinola felt the King wanted to exercise control over one entity rather than have his authority diluted by two powerful transnational orders. No less an authority than Dante called Philip the "new Pilate" in his Il Purgatorio (xx, 91)—a strange analogy since unlike Christ's persecutor, the King, according to Dante himself, was motivated by cupidity rather than Pilate's political expediency. In the "Canto" of the Divine Comedy that described the fate of the avaricious, Dante accused the French King, not the Templars, of greed. Not only had Philip persecuted two successive Popes, the Florentine poet complained, but he had also "lawlessly brought his greedy sails into the very Temple itself."

Florence at the time seems to have been a hotbed of papal gadflies and royal francophobes. Boccaccio added his criticism and verse to the polemics of his colleague in Florence, as did their compatriot and contemporary, the Florentine chronicler Giovanni Villani. When Philip sought support and moral justification from the local intelligentsia he presumed he controlled, they showed an academic independence that shames all the other voices who abandoned the venerated order and questions excuses based on self-preservation. When asked by the King for their opinion, the theologians at the University of Paris gave it—and sided with the Pope. Philip was in violation of canonical law for ordering the arrest and examination of the Templars by the secular arm rather than by Holy Mother Church. The scholars conceded that Philip had the right to arrest religious wrongdoers, but final judgement had to be rendered in ecclesiastical, not secular, courts. Philip continued to insist on royal jurisdiction, not wanting to risk an adverse verdict in a religious arena that might be biased toward fellow members of the cloth.

Before ordering the arrests, the King claimed he had conferred with and received approval from the Pope, the hierarchy of the French church, and all his nobles. Their acquiescence was not surprising. The Pope remained a "Babylonian captive" at Avignon, and both the religious and secular magnates coveted land, which their pious predecessors had squandered on the Templars in what must have now seemed like laughable superstition to the progressive medievals.

In an era of primitive communications, the seizure of the Templars was coordinated and executed with a precision that bordered on the supernatural. On October 13, 1307, bailiffs and jurists called seneschals, armed to the teeth, showed up at every Templar monastery in France and seized the warrior monks, who all surrendered without a fight, suggesting that criticism of their luxurious lifestyle was justified and had made these one-time scourges of Islam soft.

Philip seems to have felt himself on shaky ground. The approval of the papacy and the French was not enough for the nervous ruler. He wrote to all his royal coevals, urging them to follow his example and arrest their Templars. A secret agent named Bernard Peletin carried a letter from Philip to the newly crowned King of England, Edward II, with more explicit descriptions of the Templars' perversions, which delicacy had apparently stopped him from including in his bailiffs' arrest orders. Edward took action immediately. He sent Peletin back to his master with a letter saying that the charges were preposterous and unbelievable and there would be no simultaneous assault on the Temple across the Channel. But in case his incredulity turned out to be unjustified, Edward added that he would begin his own investigation and promised to stay in touch with his royal brother.

Undeterred, Philip mounted a public relations campaign on the home front. Monks acting like the equivalent of medieval spin doctors were appointed to deliver sermons in town squares throughout France, elaborating and embroidering the original charges used to arrest the Templars. Their idolatry was described in detail. They worshipped an embalmed idol covered with an animal skin. "In this idol there were two carbuncles for eyes, bright as the brightness of heaven, and it is certain that all the hope of the Templars was placed in it. It was their sovereign god, and they trusted in it with all their heart," the monks proclaimed in their sermons. No wonder that King Edward, despite his own yearning for the wealth of the Temple, scoffed at this and other accusations that fueled Philip's offensive.

Cremation was a Christian taboo until the twentieth century, and the Templars were accused of burning the corpses of their departed colleagues. Cremation was not a serious enough charge for Philip, so he threw in cannibalism! The ashes of the dead were mixed into the food and drink of the monks, the King charged.

The medieval *bête noire* of burning babies, often used to justify pogroms against another wealthy minority, the Jews, was also ascribed to the Templars. After being roasted alive, the infants were eaten. The Templars also deflowered nubile virgins and committed a "variety of abominations too absurd and horrible to be named," the Victorian Charles Addison claimed, although he was actually too embarrassed to describe one of the other "absurd abominations," which was homosexuality. Too embarrassed to describe in English, that is. Addison was too conscientious a scholar not to provide a full account, so in his *The History of the Knights Templars*, published in 1842, he quoted a contemporary chronicler, Guillaume Paradin, *in French*, apparently hoping that his Victorian readers were not bilingual. To make sure, the quotation was in Middle French, which even bilingual readers would be unable to decipher, just as modern students of Chaucer find the Middle English of *The Canterbury Tales* almost unintelligible. Addison's bowdlerized text obliquely quoted testimony referring to "*femmes et fils seduites pour etre de ce secte . . .*" ("women and boys, seduced into joining the order . . .")

The first accusation of homosexual practices was made not by the King but by a close associate, his chief prosecutor, a royal judge of bourgeois birth named Guillaume de Nogaret. For the first time, in 1308, during the royal and papal assembly at Poitiers, de Nogaret introduced the charge of homosexuality by quoting no less an authority than Saladin, who claimed the Templars had not only done homage to him but attributed their failure in battle to the corrupting effects of sodomy. In the 1990s, Peter Partner felt confident enough to summarize the historical consensus as considering the allegations of homosexuality "pure invention." De Molay declared himself "stupefied" by Nogaret's allegation and implied by his amazement that it was the first he had heard of practices he would first deny, then admit only after torture, followed by a final recantation.

The philanthropy and piety of the Templars were too well known to be ignored or sullied by tall tales allegedly told by Saladin. The preacher monks hired to demonize the Templars acknowledged the Templars' favorable reputation, but managed to turn virtue into vice, anticipating Pope's famous phrase, "damning with faint praise." The Templars, their accusers explained, "to conceal the iniquity of their lives . . . made much almsgiving, constantly frequented church, comported themselves with edification, frequently partook of the holy sacrament, and manifested always much modesty and gentleness of deportment in the house, as well as in public."

They might have been idolatrous cannibals of babies, but the Templars knew how to put up a good front.

After twelve horrific days of examination under torture, not a single member of the order confessed. They were then handed over to their bitter rivals and fellow monks, the Dominicans, whom a nineteenth-century observer described as "the most refined and expert torturers of the day."

As they did in Spain and Italy, the Dominicans staffed the French Inquisition, and their Grand Inquisitor continued the barbarous pretrial depositions, adding insult to injury by conducting them on the victims' home turf, the Paris Temple.

The Dominicans lived up to their reputation as lethal interrogators. One hundred and forty Templars underwent interrogation so brutal that thirty-six died after several weeks in the Dominicans' custody. The Templars proved as stoic under torture as they had been fearless in battle, and although some confessed, they all eventually recanted.

The Victorian historian Charles Addison felt squeamish about mentioning the accusations of homosexuality, but he did not hold back when describing the torture in detail. While an iron pillory immobilized their legs, the victims' feet were first swabbed with animal fat or butter, then put to the torch. A handheld fan regulated

IBERIAN CALVARY: A Templar recreation of Christ's crucifixion was erected in Cardenosa, near Avila, Spain, in the thirteenth century. (*David Lees*)

the flame to increase or decrease the intensity of the heat depending on the degree of the victim's cooperation. This ingenious calibration of pain drove some of the monks mad. Many of the Templars were permanently crippled by the ordeal. One Templar, Bernarde de Vado, broke under torture, but recanted and was turned over to a secular official. The monk offered the official grisly proof to explain why he had confessed. "They held me so long before a fierce fire that the flesh was burnt off my heels, two pieces of bone came away, which I present to you," he told his gaoler. Another Templar explained that he confessed in order to save the remainder of his teeth, after four of them were torn out.

The Dominicans also used psychological torture. They showed the Templars forged letters from the Grand Master confessing his crimes and urging his subordinates to follow their leader's example. The physical abuse proved ineffective, but the forgeries appeared to have crushed the Templars' morale, and some who had been unpersuaded by fire confessed after reading the letters.

Unlike his Victorian counterpart, the twentieth-century historian Peter Partner didn't bother to describe the Templars' torture, which may explain why he criticized the speed with which de Molay and his subordinates confessed.

Unlike modern armchair stoics such as Partner, Europeans at the time were repelled by the scandalous treatment of the Templars. Although the King of England did not mind robbing the order of its wealth, he held the line at torture. A month after the inquisition had begun in Paris, Edward II sent letters to the Kings of Portugal, Castile, Aragon, and Sicily, denouncing the King of France. Edward wrote that the French King's agent, Bernard Peletin, had arrived at his court with documents that attempted to prove the Templars guilty of "enormities repugnant to the Catholic faith." Citing the order's faithful service in Palestine and its "becoming devotion to God," Edward declared the documents a cynical hoax. He also mentioned that similar accusations had never been made against the order during their two-century-long existence until now. The English King begged the recipients of his letter to turn "a deaf ear to the slanders of ill-natured men," and suggested the real reason for the slander was "cupidity and envy." Edward urged his royal brothers not to confiscate Templar property in their kingdoms until, and unless, a fair trial without torture proved him wrong.

Edward also sent a letter to Pope Clement, recommending that he conduct an independent inquiry. But the Pope remained the King of France's creature and captive in Avignon. Before Edward's letter reached him,

Clement had already issued a papal bull addressed to the order's defender in England. Clement claimed that the charges were not new, despite Edward's claim. The Pope had been hearing rumors of "perfidious apostasy [and] detestable heretical depravity" for years. The sly pontiff did admit the Templars' reputation as holy warriors and pious monks made him skeptical of the rumors at first.

So, what changed the Pope's mind about their guilt? Ironically, it was the same thing that had made Edward dismiss the accusations. Clement cited the confessions extracted under torture as proof of their crimes. The Pope ordered the King of England to follow the King of France's lead and seize every Templar in his kingdom and confiscate all their property.

Edward's greed overcame his sense of fair play, and the wealth of the order proved an irresistible temptation. Although the Pope suggested in his bull that Templar property and liquid assets should be held in escrow by "certain trustworthy persons" during the investigations and trials, Edward decided he was the most trustworthy person in his Kingdom. The order's lands and movable goods were inventoried, and caretakers were hired to farm their lands during the monks' imprisonment so the King would not lose the harvest, which was now his.

Edward sent his letter of protest to the Pope on November 20, 1307. A month later, he sent secret writs to every sheriff in England ordering arrests and confiscations, emphasizing that the sheriffs were only custodians of the property, which belonged to the King. Edward was not only greedy, but also thorough. Similar instructions went out to Scotland and Ireland. The writs were sealed with orders not to execute them until they were opened on January 8, 1308. Similar to Philip's lightning strike in France, all the Templars in England, Ireland, and Scotland were arrested on the same day, an amazing feat of coordination in an age of primitive communications and glacial travel.

William de la More, the master of the London Temple and the top official in the British Isles, along with the other monks in the capital, was placed under "close custody" in Canterbury Castle. Showing an independence from secular authority which his papal superior lacked, the Bishop of Durham ordered the King to free de la More on bail.

In August, Clement issued another bull, "*Faciens Misericordiam,*" addressed to the Archbishop of Canterbury and other English ecclesiastics, rehashing the same arguments he had made to the King of England. Yes, the Pope was suspicious at first because of the Templars' piety in peace and ferociousness in holy war, but the King of France had convinced him of their guilt, even though it had been admitted under torture.

There was one striking difference between the papal bull issued to Edward and the one his clergy received from the Pope. Cynics were already saying that greed was the real motive for the witch-hunt, and Clement used the bull to deny the allegation.

"Our most dear son in Christ, Philip, the illustrious King of the French, not from motives of avarice (since he does not design to apply or to appropriate to himself any portion of the estates of the Templars, nay, has washed his hands of them!), but inflamed with zeal for the orthodox faith," the Pope declared in his bull, had supplied him with irrefutable proof of the monks' guilt. Clement was either misinformed or being disingenuous. The bankrupt Philip had indeed expropriated all the Templar wealth in his Kingdom.

By now, Edward had also seized the Templar loot. Clement decided to condemn the English King's greed while ignoring his French master's, since he was Philip's captive. Edward received a letter from the Pope chastising him for the same malfeasance committed by his colleague across the Channel. The Pope also wanted his cut of the bonanza. Clement complained that Edward was distributing Templar lands to cronies and announced that he was sending emissaries to England to take possession of the forfeited property in the Pontiff's name. The papal commissioners would also serve as inquisitors of the accused Templars, since the Pope feared the King of England might not be as adept at extracting confessions under torture as the King of France and the Dominicans had been. An English trial and acquittal would create a scandal even the sophist Pope could not paper over with papal bulls.

Edward's dismissive reply to Clement's criticism and orders suggest his low regard for the papacy. Edward proved himself a master of Orwellian *doublespeak* when he wrote the Pope denying his confiscation of the Templars' wealth: "As to the goods of the Templars, we have done nothing with them up to the present time, nor do we intend to do with them aught but what we have a right to do, and what we know will be acceptable *to the Most High*." Edward's insolence has the ring of proto-Protestantism as he goes over the head of the Pope and deals directly with his boss.

Edward backed off a bit and allowed two papal inquisitors from France, the Abbot of Lagny and the Canon of Narbonne, to come to England and interrogate the Templars. But he obviously did not trust the inquisitors because he ordered the Archbishop of Canterbury and the Bishops of London and Lincoln "to be personally present" during the interrogations by the French prelates.

In all, 229 Templars were imprisoned in various castle dungeons throughout the kingdom. Many escaped, slipped into secular clothes, and hid in the wilds of Scotland, Ireland, and Wales. The English chief, William de la More, who had been free on bail, was sent to the Tower of London by order of the King, along with high-ranking members of the order including the treasurer, who it was hoped might reveal hidden Templar wealth under torture, and Himbert Blanke, an internationally known military hero who had survived the fall of Acre only to end up "for his meritorious and memorable services in defence of the Christian faith in a dungeon in the Tower," as one contemporary chronicler wrote.

After the imprisonment of the Templar hierarchy, what little remained of their property that had not been confiscated by the King began to fall into the hands of freelance expropriators. Proving himself every bit as greedy as his counterpart in France, Edward sent two investigators to find the thieves, retrieve the loot, and bring the miscreants to trial.

The fate of the Templars did not look promising. Before a single prisoner was interrogated, the Archbishop of Canterbury, acting on the Pope's orders, had Clement's bull read in every church in England on September 22, 1309. In the bull, the Pope reflected the medieval concept of jurisprudence that the accused was guilty until proven innocent. The Pope said he was already convinced of the Templars' guilt and threatened to excommunicate anyone who disagreed with him. As for the Templars remaining at large, anyone who sheltered or even showed them "kindness or counsel" would also suffer excommunication.

The papal inquisitors arrived in England the first week of October, bringing with them a list of the charges, which were read to the prisoners in the Tower, who had languished there for almost two years.

On October 22, 1309, the papal inquisitors joined various English and French prelates at the Episcopal palace of the Bishop of London to read the charges, eighty-seven in all, which the historian Charles Addison with Gibbonesque flair castigated as a "monument of human folly, superstition, and credulity."

The alleged crimes had a boring and suspicious similarity to the ones committed by the Templars in France. As part of their initiation rite, the Templars were required to deny the divinity of Christ, spit on a crucifix, then trample it. Some of the charges seem lightweight compared to others, but in an era of superstition, the accusation, for example, that Templar priests did not say the words that turned bread and wine into the body and blood of Christ during Mass may have been more shocking then than now. Article 30 of the charges spelled out the homosexual practices of the order, but the Victorian historian Addison again resorts to an ellipsis when recording them since, this time, he cannot hide behind opaque Middle French: "That in receiving brothers into the order, or when about to receive them, or some time after having received them, the receivers and the persons received kissed one another on the mouth, the navel . . . !!!" Addison deleted "anus" and added the exclamation points.

The horrified Victorian scholar confesses his act of bowdlerization and refuses to repeat Articles 39 through 45, which contained "crimes and abominations too horrible and disgusting to be named." The remaining, less salty articles mostly revolved around the worship of various idols, including the human skull described in the French testimony.

Twentieth-century historians are more forthcoming about the homosexual aspects of the initiation rite, which medieval contemporaries had no problem recording for posterity at length and in detail, leading Victorians to an orgy of self-censorship. Postulants had to swear to grant sexual favors to other members of the order in order to become full-fledged monks. Beside sacrilegious, the initiation rite sounds exhausting since it involved kissing so many parts of the body, including the exposed back, the navel, the mouth, the lower spine, and finally the idol Baphomet, which was a variant spelling of Mohammed. Depending on the confession, the image of Baphomet resembled a cat and was inspired by the *maufe* or demon of French folklore, who was a recurring character in tales of witchcraft and heresy. Although many Templars denied idolatry, those who confessed outdid their accusers' imagination and the idol took on as many forms as the number of guilty. To some, the idol was a skull, others a reliquary, a cat, several cats, a painting on a wall or on a wooden beam, or the head of a man with the Templars' signature long beard. The idol became a fashion accessory in some accounts, worn at the girdle and attached by a cord. Despite its unusual appearance, the idol never drew attention until the Templars' trials. When it was not being used for sexual pleasure or initiation, the idol served more practical purposes, according to some testimony. In an era plagued by famine, the idol was said to have a magical ability that caused trees to grow and plants to flower. The idol and all its myriad incarnations became a Rorschach stained glass window that reflected the creativity of the victims and the effectiveness of their torturers. While the object of worship mutated, the monotonous and repetitious name for it—Baphomet—in most confessions suggested, according to Peter Partner, a common source: the prosecution rather than the prosecuted. According to the charges, the idol originated in Islam, a preposterous notion since Mohammed forbade the veneration of any graven image, and no Islamic chroniclers ever mentioned their co-religionists engaging in its worship. Part of an inventive smear campaign, the idol reflected Christian imagery rather than Islamic. Despite the injunction against idol worship, such worship throughout the history of both faiths was attributed by one to the other as the worst form of insult—much as pedophilia is used today in everything from child custody battles to preschool witch-hunts such as the McMartin case.

As the accusations grew, so did the number of body parts and bodily functions involved in the order's initiation rites. Besides kissing each other on the anus and penis, they were accused of kissing the same parts of the idol. In addition to spitting on the crucifix, the list of crimes came to include urinating and defecating on Christ's image. Nothing was left to the imagination of the faithful in the prosecutors' zeal to stir it up.

Four hundred years later the atheist and anticlerical Voltaire dismissed the list with almost as much contempt as the Templars' Victorian champion Addison did. The French philosopher riposted, "Such accusations destroyed themselves."

Addison's French contemporary, Jules Michelet, was less dismissive of the charges against the Templars and hypothesized that there may have been a kernel of truth in the accounts publicized during the Templars' show trials. But, according to Michelet, their behavior was based on reverence, not sacrilege, since the renunciations recreated St. Peter's denial of Christ in the Bible and did not represent a profane denial of Jesus' divinity. In *The Papacy and the Ruin of the Templars*, the German historian Heinrich Finke absolved the Templars of all heresies and claimed that they were fabricated by a corrupt judiciary, papacy, and various royals. Modern day historian Matthew Barber also maintains their innocence, while his contemporary Jean Favrier said in his biography of King Philip that the Templars did engage in such holy acts, but attributes their behavior to ignorance and mediocrity on the part of the order's leadership rather than profound irreligiosity or sexual malfeasance among the rank and file.

Unfortunately for the Templars, their persecutors did not share Voltaire's or later historians' philosophies.

After hearing the charges, William de la More and thirty of his subordinates denied them all and claimed their brothers in France had perjured themselves when they confessed to similar crimes.

One by one, the Templars repeated the nature of the actual initiation rite, which consisted of commendable things like vows of chastity and poverty. They all demonstrated a wily sense of self-preservation by adding that the initiation included a promise to "succour the Holy Land with all [their] might and defend it against the enemies of the Christian faith," reminding their accusers of the greatest source of their international acclaim. During his examination, the Templar Thomas le Chamberleyn insisted that the English initiation rite was identical to rites practiced by the order throughout Europe, but in a fatal admission added that no laypersons were allowed to attend the ceremony. The inquisitors jumped on that admission and demanded to know the reason for such secrecy. The Templar was unable to give a reason. Himbert Blanke, the war hero from Acre and second-highest ranking Templar in France, happened to be in England when the Templars were seized, and he found himself in the English dock. Asked why their initiation rite had been closed to the public, Blanke realized the giant loophole his brother Thomas le Chamberleyn had opened up and sadly replied, "Through our own unaccountable folly." A member of the order for almost forty years, Blanke denied all the charges and reiterated the accusation of his fellow prisoners: If the Grand Master of the Temple in France had confessed to the crimes, he was lying. Blanke's accusation had special gravity because the Templars were famous for obedience to their leader, whom one of their most senior members now denounced as a perjurer.

Seven witnesses who were not members of the order testified on November 19 and 20, but the purpose of their testimony continues to mystify since they were not Templars and could only supply at best—or worst—innuendo about the initiation rites these "witnesses" were not allowed to witness. A notary public, Master William le Dorturer, testified that he "thought the secrecy of the rite was owing to a bad rather than a good motive," but had to concede he had never witnessed the results of the "bad motive." Three witnesses, a former messenger who worked for the London Temple, a priest named Richard de Barton, and Radulph de Rayndon, identified only as "an old man," all testified that they had heard only good things about the order in England. The desperate papal inquisitors were grasping at straws.

The interrogations at the Bishop of London's palace were going nowhere, and at the order of the Pope, the Archbishop of Canterbury assembled a council of high-ranking clergy and university theologians at St. Paul's

Cathedral for the purpose of absolving or condemning the Templars.

Another papal bull declaring the Pope's presumption of the Templars' guilt and a detailed description of their crimes were read aloud at the convocation. After six days of debate, the prelates petitioned the King to oust the papal inquisitors and grant the English clergy the right to try the accused in ecclesiastical courts. The motion amounted to a public slap in the face of papal oversight and prestige and must have resounded throughout the Kingdom. It resonated with King Edward, who granted the council's request.

Meanwhile, members of the Scottish branch of the order were being interrogated at the Church of the Holy Cross in Edinburgh with similar results. The Scottish Templars all repeated the reverential nature of the initiation rite and refused to confess to any of the alleged abominations. Forty-one witnesses, among them abbots, priests, monks, and servants of the Templars, testified against the order, but like their counterparts at the English hearings, all they could add was innuendo. While other monastic orders performed their investitures in public and with pomp, the secrecy of the Templars' initiation made these witnesses suspect the worst without being able to justify their suspicions with evidence. New charges not in the papal bull surfaced at these hearings, but hearsay predominated over hard facts. The Abbot of the Holy Cross Church in Edinburgh accused the Templars of stealing the property of neighbors. The Abbot of Dumferlyn admitted he had no firsthand knowledge of that accusation, but insisted he had "*heard* much and *suspected* more." Templar servants who were not members of the order and did not participate in their initiation rites, along with peasant farmers who worked Templar lands, only confirmed the old complaint that their masters' rituals were held in secrecy. Even secondhand hearsay was offered at the hearings. Some witnesses reported they had heard "old men" speculate that if the Templars had been good Christians they would not have lost the Holy Land, which seemed to beg the question that the failure of the Crusades was caused by the warrior monks in the first place and repeated the canard that began with the fall of Acre.

Under the new jurisdiction of the English clergy, the investigation of the Templars resumed in January 1310 at the church of St. Dunstan's West. The case against the order had become so weak, witnesses undercut their own testimony. The Rector of the church of St. Mary de la Strode insisted that he had "strong suspicions" that the accused were guilty of the grotesque acts performed during their initiation rites, but unlike the Templars' servants in Scotland, the Rector had actually been present at some of these rites and admitted he had seen nothing untoward. The Vicar of St. Martin's-in-the Fields, a priest from St. Clement's Church, and many other London clergymen, all testified that they had no personal or secondhand knowledge of crimes committed by the Templars. Later that month, at a hearing in the chapel of the Blessed Mary of Berkyngeschere in London, a servant of the Templars suggested they were conscientious about policing malfeasance in their own ranks. John de Stoke, who had served the monks for almost twenty years, described the unusual burial service of an errant member. The deceased had been imprisoned by the order for two months before his death after confessing to stealing Templar property. The culprit, Walter le Bachelor, had been excommunicated and buried without the Templar habit. The Templars were strict, but merciful. Just before his death, le Bachelor's excommunication was lifted, he confessed his sins to a priest of the order, and was allowed to receive Holy Communion and Extreme Unction. In an age when the belief in hellfire was vivid and real, the clemency shown by the order to its wayward member on his deathbed was both impressive and generous.

During the first week of February, at hearings held in churches scattered throughout London, thirty-four more Templars swore that the papal accusations, especially the alleged blasphemy during initiations, had never occurred. These Templars added that their leader in France, Jacques de Molay, and his second in command, the Grand Preceptor, lied when they confessed to having committed such acts.

On March 1, as the case against the Templars continued to weaken, the King sent orders to their places of confinement that they were to be kept in separate cells, in an apparent attempt to prevent them from coordinating their testimony. The conditions of their imprisonment must have been harsh. During hearings on March 3 at the Bishop of London's palace and at several churches, Templars mentioned during their interrogation that a number of their order had died in captivity. New accusations were made at these hearings that the Templars buried their dead in secret. No misconduct was alleged, but the need for secrecy implied that something objectionable must have occurred. Refuting this innocuous charge, the head of the order in England, William de la More, Master of the London Temple, pointed out that parishioners from nearby churches often attended internment ceremonies at the order's headquarters.

In Ireland, a risible hearing at Saint Patrick's Church in Dublin anticipated Voltaire's claim that history repeats itself—first as tragedy, the second time as farce. After thirty Templars refused to admit any wrongdoing, witnesses for the prosecution admitted that their accusations were based on hearsay and suspicion. The Dublin allegations were minor compared to the charges of blasphemy and homosexuality leveled in England and France. Forty-one Irish witnesses, mostly monks, testified that they noticed that the Templars were *inattentive* during church sermons and stared at the ground during the consecration and elevation of the Eucharist at Mass.

By the end of March, the case against the Templars had almost collapsed. The desperate King relented and allowed the more efficient inquisitors appointed by the Pope to take charge of investigations conducted at the Cathedral Church in Lincoln. The well-known viciousness of the papal legates may have appealed to the King as a counterweight to the fame and repute of the Templars who were interrogated at Lincoln. Internationally known military heroes of the Crusades, who had the added venerability of great age, testified that the initiation rites they attended in England were the same as those performed throughout Europe and Palestine, including France, and that none of the sacrileges confessed to in France had occurred anywhere. During the French interrogations, some Templars confessed to wearing unspecified undergarments or girdles that suggested fetishism. At Lincoln, one of the old warriors, Robert de Hamilton, admitted that the knights wore the undergarments, but the clothing represented an act of piety and reminded the audience of the service performed by the order in defense of the Holy Land. The girdles had been pressed against a shrine to the Virgin Mary at Nazareth and were worn by Templars as relics, not fetishes. With all the gravity of his age and military fame, de Hamilton branded his fellow monks in France liars for attaching a salacious significance to the girdles.

During a hearing at York in May, the Templar Stephen de Radenhall fueled suspicion about the initiation rite. Unlike his brothers, who described the rite in detail to prove its innocence, de Radenhall refused to discuss the ritual, claiming he had been sworn to secrecy on pain of losing membership in the order and imprisonment. No other Templars reported similar oaths.

The smear campaign against the Templars continued with a boring recapitulation of accusations that everyone in the England, Scotland, and Ireland must have already heard. After celebrating Mass at the Cathedral in York on May 20, the Archbishop ordered the original papal bulls against the Templars to be read again.

In June, the Pope's henchmen resumed hearings at Lincoln and demonstrated a morbid interest in a new area of Templar protocol, their self-imposed penitential rites, which until now had not generated any accusations of inappropriate behavior—or worse. It appears that the Templars were their own worst critics—at least until the King of France surpassed their zeal. Sixteen Templars testified that the typical punishment suffered by penitents was three lashes with a leather whip, applied to their bare backs. With nothing more sensational to uncover, the papal inquisitors wrapped up the Lincoln hearings in a week and moved on to London, where the Master of the Order in England, William de la More, was called to testify again, along with thirty-eight fellow knights, chaplains, and squires. Their interrogators seemed obsessed with the Templars' self-chastisement and ordered de la More to describe the floggings *in detail.* A modern day psychologist might be forgiven for finding elements of voyeurism and *ecouteurism* in the inquisitors' obsessive quest for the seamy particulars of penance meted out by the order to wayward members.

The examiners ordered de la More to repeat the precise words he used while flogging sinners. If his persecutors were hoping for some kind of fiendish expression of sadism while de la More administered punishment, they must have been disappointed by the Master's white bread account. "Brother, pray to God that He may forgive you," de la More told the penitent and ordered the monks who witnessed the beating, "And do ye, brothers, beseech the Lord to forgive him his sins, and say a *Pater Noster*." Then he admonished the sinner not to make the same mistake again. De la More was not a priest, and he was accused of performing the sacrament of absolution after punishing the sinner. De la More denied appropriating priestly functions and simply told the penitent he forgave him "as far as he was able." In a rare failure of solidarity, another Templar contradicted de la More's account and claimed that the Master used the words only priests were allowed to say when granting absolution: "I forgive you in the name of the Father, and of the Son, and of the Holy Ghost." However, according to this Templar, to make sure the absolution was legitimate in a superstitious era where forgiveness meant the difference between heaven and hell, de la More then sent the penitent to a Templar priest, whom no one disputed had the right to administer the sacrament.

At the end of the hearings in London, the Pope's representatives composed a memorandum claiming that the testimony of the Templars and witnesses proved that the accused practiced rituals which were not consistent with the orthodox faith. The memorandum failed to describe the rituals or explain why they were unorthodox, no doubt because the hearings had not uncovered any evidence of heterodoxy.

The English hearings failed to extract any dramatic confessions, and the members of the English order were able to maintain their innocence despite repeated interrogations and harsh prison conditions for the simple reason that the machinery of the English inquisition, unlike in France, was not oiled with horrific tortures.

Historians remain perplexed by the dramatic difference between the *modus operandi* of the English and French proceedings against the order. King Edward may not have been as greedy and desperate as his bankrupt royal brother across the Channel, but for whatever reasons, he forbade torture of the Templars. English common law also frowned on torture in the judicial process, while common law didn't exist in fourteenth-century France, only royal fiat.

Besides common decency and the dubious authenticity of confessions extorted by pain, over the centuries, torture disappeared for the simple reason that its effectiveness was evanescent, as demonstrated by the behavior of the French Templars as soon as their tormentors freed them. Throughout the Kingdom, in the capital and the provinces, they all retracted their confessions to a man.

A furious Philip rounded up as many of these "recidivists" as he could and hauled them before an ecclesiastical tribunal, to give a religious veneer and justification to his rage. At the command of the King, the Archbishop of Sens, another royal puppet like the Pope, condemned the recusants to death. At a tribunal in Paris, the Archbishop justified the sentence by telling the condemned, "You have avowed that the brethren who are received into the order of the Temple are compelled to renounce Christ and spit upon the cross, and that you yourselves have participated in that crime. You have thus acknowledged that you have fallen into the sin of heresy." Heresy was actually a new allegation that had not been proven or admitted by the French Templars, but the order's persecutors never worried about consistency or precedent when they reached into their grab-bag of accusations. The Archbishop continued, "By your confession and repentance you had merited absolution, and had once more become reconciled to the church. As you have revoked your confession, the church no longer regards you as reconciled, but as having fallen back to your first errors. You are therefore relapsed heretics and as such, we condemn you to the fire."

Justice, or at least the grotesque French conception of it, was swift. On May 12, 1310, only one day after the Archbishop sentenced them to death, the Church handed over fifty-four Templars to the secular authorities. Royal bailiffs escorted the condemned men to a field in the Parisian suburb of Porte St. Antoine des Champs, where they were burnt at the stake. The King's vengeance was cruel. To increase the victims' agony, he ordered various combustible materials placed close to the stakes, so the Templars would be burned alive rather than perish from smoke inhalation, the more typical cause of death since kindling wood was usually dampened or ignited further away from the condemned as an act of mercy. Despite the extensive propaganda against the order promulgated by the Pope, clergy, and the King of France, eyewitnesses praised the dying monks for their stoic behavior during the grisly executions.

Not all members of the order in France had cracked under torture. After the *auto-da-fé* on the outskirts of Paris, the Archbishop of Sens dragged the Templars who had refused to confess from their dungeons, condemned them to life imprisonment, then sent them back to prison. The bravery and integrity of both the Templars who refused to confess and those who retracted their confessions were underlined by the happier fate of those who admitted guilt and stuck to their story. They received absolution and readmission to the Church and were set free. But despite the ghastly consequences, Templars throughout France continued to retract their confessions.

The fiery executions dragged on into August and spread from Paris to Lorraine, Normandy, Carcassone, and Senlis. A total of 113 Templars perished in the capital, but the number of victims in the provinces went unrecorded.

The King's fury toward the order degenerated from merely pathological to necrophiliac. His officers exhumed the corpse of the former treasurer of the Paris Temple and consigned it to the flames.

Amid the executions, the grim work of the inquisitors continued. The treatment of the aged members of the order, who had once been feted military heroes of the glorious wars against the infidel, was particularly pitiful. Described by observers as trembling and panic-stricken, these fading old soldiers refused to die. Already near death from the ravages of imprisonment and old age, they summoned the courage for one last assault on their tormentors and retracted their confessions, which meant certain death. Their courage deserted them, however, and they begged for another hearing, where they retracted their retractions, admitted their guilt once again, and begged for forgiveness, which, despite so many *volte-faces*, was granted. Humiliated and disgraced, the once proud warriors were set free.

Younger Templars were more recalcitrant. At the Chateau d'Alaix, four prisoners died under torture, but twenty more confessed to new crimes which injected a supernatural and diabolical element into the order's alleged rituals. Besides the old charge of worshipping the head of an idol, for the first time the monks testified that the devil had appeared to them in the shape of a talking cat that promised them a bountiful harvest, more land, and valuables. The Templars failed to coordinate their stories, with some describing the idol's head as an old man's with a long beard, while others claimed it had the face of a beautiful woman. Still others confessed that many devils appeared during their ceremonies, but instead of the cat, they assumed the form of beautiful women.

In England, the Templars continued to maintain their innocence, and the Pope knew why. In June 1310, Clement sent a letter to King Edward, condemning his unwillingness to use torture and specifically ordering him to start using the rack. The English clergy began to put pressure on the King to employ the French method. After holding out for two months, Edward relented and gave up custody of the Templars, who were imprisoned in the Tower of London. He ordered the Constable of the Tower, John de Crumbewell, to transfer the prisoners to various jails in the city controlled by the papal inquisitors and gave them carte blanche to use torture. Another reason for Edward's about-face is suggested by the debt-ridden King's order that the Pope's men would have to pay for the upkeep of the Templars in their custody.

The English clergy were not as bloodthirsty as their papal and French counterparts, and their squeamishness was reflected in a curious decree issued in London on September 21 during a public interrogation of the Templars. After violent debates, the prelates agreed to the use of torture if the Templars refused to confess, but stipulated that "perpetual mutilation or disabling of any limb" was forbidden as well as the "violent effusion of blood."

The civil authorities shared the clergy's temperance. Four months after Edward ordered their transfer, the Constable of the Tower still had not turned over his prisoners to the papal inquisitors. Charles Addison wrote, "The [Tower] gaolers of these unhappy gentlemen seem to have been more merciful and considerate than their judges, and to have manifested the greatest reluctance to act upon the orders sent from the King." Edward's apologetic letter of October 23 to the Constable of the

Tower served to remind him that the King was only act-ing out of respect for the Pope. A compromise was reached when Edward agreed to keep the Templars in the Tower, but allow the papal inquisitors to summon them at will for interrogation (and torture).

Edward's guilt about the shabby treatment of the Templars is suggested by a letter he addressed to the city's citizens, and sent a month later (November 22) to the Mayor of London. In the message, he explained that by ordering the use of torture, he was complying with the Pope's commands. Inexplicably, he also announced that he would continue to pay the Templars' expenses, even though they were under the control of the Pope's representatives. The following week, the King tempered his mercy with misery. On December 12, he ordered the Templars imprisoned in Lincoln to be transferred to London. They were to be placed in solitary confinement in various prisons operated by the Mayor throughout the city, but not in the Tower, where the sympathies of its Constable remained suspect. And for the first time, the King added the humiliation of putting the proud knights in irons and on starvation rations. While the Mayor had physical custody of the prisoners, the papal inquisitors were granted free access to them by the King and "allowed to torture the bodies of the Templars in any way that they might think fit."

After three years of imprisonment, including three months of torture, starvation, solitary confinement, and a freezing English winter, the Templars, it was presumed, had been softened up enough to appear before the Pope's examiners and the Bishops of London and Chichester at two London venues—the Churches of St. Martin's, Ludgate, and St. Botoph's, Bishopsgate, on March 30, 1311. Their tormentors' presumption that degradation and despair would make the victims more pliable turned out to be false. Despite torture and a guarantee of freedom if they confessed, every single prisoner refused and reasserted his innocence at these hearings. The enraged tribunal ordered them back to prison for more torture and heavier fetters.

Since the Templars refused to incriminate themselves, their judges resorted to the less compelling testimony of so-called witnesses, who provided hearsay and gossip, but few firsthand accounts. Many of the seventy-two witnesses were members of rival monastic orders—Carmelites, Augustinians, Dominicans, and Minorites.

An Irish monk, Henry Thanet, without identifying his sources, testified he had heard that the Templar Hugh de Nipurias had deserted the order in Palestine and converted to Islam. The witness claimed that the Templar commander of the Pilgrim's Castle in the Holy

Land had ordered new members to deny Christ during the initiation rite, but the accuser was unable to name the commander or the inductees. The Irishman added he had heard of another, unnamed Templar who owned a talking, two-faced idol made of bronze that had the power to answer all questions.

Borrowing a page from the Bible, John de Nassington swore that two Templar knights, Milo de Stapleton and Adam de Everington, worshipped a calf during an annual feast at the monastery of Templehurst in England.

Sir John de Eure, the Sheriff of York, recounted a dinner at his home with William de la Fenne, the head of the Templar's monastery in Wesdall. After the meal, the defendant pulled a book from under his mantle and gave it to Sir John's wife to read. Glued to a page was a separate piece of paper containing a laundry list of heresies. The document said that Jesus was not the son of God and the Virgin Mary, but the mortal offspring of Mary and Joseph; that Jesus was a false prophet cruci-fied for his sins, not mankind's; and more steamy stuff that must have burned medieval ears. Unlike the other preposterous testimony about talking cats and wor-shipping calves, there was a smattering of truth to this story. The owner of the book, William de la Fenne, was dragged out of prison and confirmed most of the details in court, including dining with his host and loaning the lady his book, but denied the existence of the piece of paper and its heretical contents. The accused noted that his accuser had waited six years to come forth with such damning information.

William de la Forde, a prominent priest and rector of a church in Crofton, Yorkshire, provided more hearsay evidence. An Augustinian priest, now dead, violated the secrecy of the confessional when he told de la Forde the sins the Templar Patrick of Rippon had confessed to him. During his initiation, Patrick had been ordered to deny the divinity of Christ, spit on a "representation" of the crucifix, and worship and kiss the image of a calf on an altar, all of which he did, "weeping bitterly."

No accusation was too petty or preposterous. A rare eyewitness testified he saw a Templar moon the altar. A Minorite monk, Robert of Oteringham, claimed that while a guest of the Templars at their monastery in Ribstane, Yorkshire, he heard a chaplain in another room scolding some noisy monks, "The devil will burn you!" The curious guest went to investigate and found a Templar engaged in behavior the Victorian historian Addison found so embarrassing that he didn't translate the original medieval Latin the testimony was recorded in: "*Brachis depositis, tenentem faciem versus occidentem et posteriora versus altare."* This is what the historian felt was too racy for his Victorian audience: "Having pulled down his pants, he turned his face to the west and his backside to the altar." The witness of that prankish scene had an excellent memory and recalled an incident that had occurred twenty years earlier. Then a guest of the Templars at another Yorkshire monastery, the witness heard noises coming from the chapel at midnight—an unusual time for a church service. Peering through a keyhole, he could not see anything suspicious and presumed from the large number of candles lit in the chapel that the monks were celebrating an important saint's feast day. The next morning, when he asked a Templar the name of the saint, the man blanched and, terrified, begged him, "Go thy way, and if you love me, or have any regard for your own life, never speak of this matter." During the same visit, when the two men were in the chapel, the witness tried to pick up a crucifix he found lying on the floor, but the Templar stopped him, saying, "Lay down the cross and depart in peace!"

After this gossipy minutiae, the inquisitors read aloud in court more serious confessions made by two members of the order in France after being put to the rack. During his initiation, Robert de St. Just confessed he had denied Christ and spat "beside" the cross. A high ranking Templar, Geoffrey de Gonville, the leader of the order in Aquitaine and Poitou, confessed that during his initiation at the Temple in London twenty-eight years earlier, the head of the English branch showed him an illustration of the crucifix in a missal and ordered him to deny Christ. The alarmed novice refused, and so the Englishman explained the reason for the order and assured him that it was not a sin. According to the Byzantine explanation, a former Grand Master held captive in the Holy Land by a sultan had instituted the custom as a condition of his release imposed by his captor. The Englishman insisted that the sacrilegious rite was actually a pious reenactment of St. Peter's denial of Christ. The novice still refused, but agreed to a compromise, promising to tell other members he had performed the ritual. During the reading of the charges, the inquisitors failed to mention that this confession had been retracted.

When another inductee refused to commit sacrilege during his initiation, he was killed, according to testimony by a secular knight, Ferinsius le Mareschal, who said that his grandfather had entered the order in London a healthy man and was dead three days later. The knight said he "suspected" his grandfather was murdered by fellow monks, but offered no proof.

An unnamed Augustinian monk swore that a Templar had told him the human soul did not exist any more than a dog's did. The rector of the church in Godmersham, identified only as Roger, swore that fifteen years earlier he had been dissuaded from entering the order by a Templar who insinuated that the initiation rite was sacrilegious, but the Templar had refused to elaborate.

The Vicar of St. Clement's Church in Sandwich testified he had heard the story of a young boy who somehow had managed to hide himself in a room where the leader of the order in England gave a sermon explaining how the Templars could acquire wealth. The witness obviously had not heard this account from the boy, who was put to the sword by a monk after the intruder revealed himself by performing a good deed. From his hiding place, the youth saw a Templar drop his girdle, which he picked up and returned to the monk, who showed his gratitude by killing him.

Even thirdhand testimony did not embarrass the voracious inquisitors. A Minorite monk, John de Gertia, said he had heard from a woman who had been told by the order's second in command in England that a Templar servant hiding in a closet saw the monks perform a ritual kiss that Charles Addison again only describes in the original Latin as *culum idoli* (i.e., the buttocks of an idol). However, one of the monks refused to participate, crying, "I was a bad man in the world and placed myself in this order for the salvation of my soul; what could I do worse? I will not do it." After the monk rejected repeated commands to perform the ritual, the Templars threw him into a well, boarded up the opening and left him to die. The witness also testified that a relative of the Earl of Warrenne had disappeared two years after entering the order and remained unaccounted for despite efforts made by members of the powerful aristocratic clan to find him.

The elaborate farce of telephone testimony—second and thirdhand accounts—continued. Another Minorite monk, John Walby de Bust, said he heard of a secret chamber in a Templar residence in London that contained the head of an idol made of gold. On his deathbed, according to this witness, one of the high ranking Templars told his subordinates that they could possess supernatural powers if they worshipped the idol.

Richard de Koefel, a monk whose order was not identified in the record of the hearing, testified that a John de Dingeston had told him that, upon entering the order, he had been told by the Templar Walter le Bacheler that every monk was required to sell his soul to the devil. The same witness said he had learned from a priest, who had been told by a vicar who was the confessor of le Bacheler, that there was a secret clause in the Templars' charter that was so outrageous it could not be revealed to "any living man."

A priest named Gasper de Nafferton, who prudently described himself as a former employee, but never a member of the order, testified that during his six-month employment he was forbidden to observe the initiation rite. When he tried to spy on the ceremony through a peephole, a Templar threatened him with death.

The Minorite John de Donygton, the seventy-sixth witness to testify during the exhaustive hearing, swore that an ancient member of the order, whose name he couldn't recall, told him that Templars had four idolatrous objects in England: one in the sacristy of the London Temple, another at their monastery in Bistelesham, another in Lincolnshire, and another whose location he couldn't remember, except that the idol was somewhere near the Humber River. The witness also alleged that the head of the English Templars, William de la More, had originated idol worship in the order and lugged around a giant scroll that contained a description of the initiation ritual in extra large letters. The ancient Templar had also told the witness that many Templars kept idols in boxes and carried them wherever they went. Kind-hearted Templars apparently tried to warn off novices, one of whom told the witness that after handing over his personal fortune, he was told by a member, "It will be the worse for you, brother, if you enter our order." When the newcomer was pressed for an explanation, his mentor said, "You see us externally, but not internally; take heed what you do; but I shall say no more." Another ancient Templar repeated the same warning to the young man.

This same witness concluded his testimony with a rambling account of a conspiracy between the order and Saracens to destroy the Christian presence in the Holy Land.

After all the witnesses had testified, senior members of the English order, including the leader, William de la More, appeared before the inquisitors at the Church of All Saints in London and presented a long declaration written in Norman French instead of Latin, so that it could be read per their request in churches throughout the Kingdom and understood by the public—or at least by English aristocrats whose first language was the French of William the Conqueror. The Templar leaders' declaration reminded its listeners of the order's long and commendable service in Palestine and denied all the heretical and sacrilegious practices of which they had been accused. At the end of the declaration, they begged their tormentors to promulgate the document exactly as written, without prosecutorial gloss or bias.

The papal inquisitors were enraged by the declaration, apparently expecting the Templar leaders, who had already confessed, to confirm their crimes at the hearing, not renounce them. They ordered the recalcitrant Templar leaders back to prison and more torture.

The King sent new orders to the monks' various gaolers throughout the city of London to increase the weight of the prisoners' chains and the severity of torture. According to an account read during another hearing, the Templars were subjected to sophisticated psychological torture, alternately treated with kindness and brutality, in what sounds like a medieval version of good cop/bad cop. Doctors of theology and high-ranking prelates also visited the Templars' dungeons and, hoping learned arguments would succeed where physical duress had failed, tried to persuade them to confess. When neither method worked, the desperate inquisitors imported French monks who had special expertise in using the rack.

While the Templar hierarchy refused to break under torture, two servants and a chaplain of the order finally confessed. On June 23, one of the servants, Stephen de Stapelbrugge, was deposed at Newgate gaol during a hearing attended by the Bishops of London and Chichester, the Archbishop of Canterbury's chancellor, and several theologians. During his testimony, de Stapelbrugge revealed there were actually two versions of the initiation rite, one sacred, the other profane. The monk testified that during his induction, two members of the order stood on either side of him with their swords drawn. Brian le Jay, the Grand Preceptor of England, ordered the novice to deny Christ and spit on the cross. Fearing for his life, the monk said he complied with the denial but made sure to miss the crucifix when he spit. At this point in his testimony, the monk knelt down and begged for forgiveness, insisting he did not care about his life, only the salvation of his soul. He knew from repeated offers that such a confession would save his life *and* his soul.

Two days later, the other servant, Thomas Tocci de Thoroldeby, appeared before the Bishops of London and Chichester, the Archdeacon of Salisbury, and other clergymen at St. Martin's Church in London. During his testimony, the man rambled on about the order's service in the Holy Land and strict adherence to the vow of poverty. An impatient inquisitor interrupted and asked if he had anything to confess. The Templar then revealed that one of the other inquisitors, the Abbot of Lagny, had visited him in gaol and threatened him with torture if he did not fabricate testimony. The accused was sent back to prison, where the Abbot made good on his threat. After four days of torture, the monk returned to the hearing and this time told a variation on the other monk's story. He confessed that he had been ordered to spit on an image of the Virgin Mary during his initiation, but instead kissed the statue's foot without managing to incur the wrath of the two Templars who brandished swords on either side of him. He also said that he had heard the Master of the London Temple deny the divinity of Christ more than 100 times and proclaim that the "smallest hair of the beard of one Saracen was worth more than the whole body of any Christian," adding that the order always hoped the Islamic cause would prevail in the Holy Land. On another occasion, when beggars asked the Master for alms in the name of the Virgin Mary, he responded, "What lady? Your lady be hanged!" then threw a ha'penny on the ground, forcing them to dig for it in the frozen winter mud.

The two Templar servants were illiterate and placed a mark instead of a signature on their confessions. The fate of the monks served as an inducement for others to comply, since they were received back into the Church after incriminating themselves during a lavish ceremony unusual for such humble men, at the Bishop of London's palace, with the Archbishop of Canterbury presiding.

Now that the head of the order in England had been incriminated, the inquisitors went after the head of the entire order, the Grand Master, Jacques de Molay. After being tortured, John de Stoke, a Templar chaplain, appeared before the Bishops of London and Chichester at St. Martin's Church on July 1, 1311. Earlier, the chaplain had insisted there was nothing irregular about his induction, but now confessed that a year later, during a visit to England, the Grand Master summoned him to his bedchamber and ordered him to sit at the foot of the bed. Again, while two Templars intimidated him with drawn swords, he was ordered to deny Christ. When the chaplain refused, the Grand Master threatened to put him in a sack and "carry him to a place which he would find by no means agreeable," adding that the two thugs in the room were ready to use their swords if necessary. The chaplain asked if everyone in the order was required to reject Christ, and the Grand Master said yes. Fearing he was about to be killed by the armed men, he complied with his leader's order.

Two days after his testimony, the chaplain repeated his confession in front of a huge crowd outside Saint Paul's cathedral that included the Archbishop of Canterbury and other high-ranking clergy. The presence of these prelates reflected the importance of the campaign to destroy the Templars' reputation.

Unlike his illiterate servant, the head of the English order could not be coerced. On July 5, the Bishop of Chichester visited William de la More in prison, with canonical lawyers and theologians to back up his threats with intellectual arguments. The Bishop ended up begging de la More, who had retracted his confession, to admit his crimes and promised absolution and freedom. De la More replied that he could not confess to crimes he had not committed, and the Bishop ordered him back to solitary confinement.

The inquisitors' run of good luck, however, continued with de la More's subordinate, a higher level witness than the terrified servants. On July 6, the Bishops of London, Winchester, and Chichester made another trip to jail, this time at Southwark, where they interrogated Philip de Mewes, head of the Templar monastery in Garwy, along with other members of the order. All of the accused changed their stories and signed a long list of heretical practices drawn up by the Bishops. The document contained the added inducement of a written guarantee of absolution.

Soon, more members of the order added their names to the confession, including the number two man in England, Michael de Baskeville, who together with seventeen other members, was received back into the Church on July 9 at the Bishop of London's palace, during a ceremony at which the hall was thrown open to the public. Some Templars, weakened by torture, were too ill for the public event, and a group of Bishops granted them absolution in a private ceremony at Saint Mary's Chapel, which was near their former place of imprisonment, the Tower of London, and lessened the travel time for the debilitated monks. The private nature of the event also prevented the public from seeing the wretched state of the Templars, which might have called into question the sincerity of their confessions. The public notary who recorded the proceedings was struck by the condition of the penitents: "They were so old and so infirm that they were unable to stand." The notary also underlined the emotional devastation of these old warriors, many of whom, he noted, were reduced to tears during their ritual humiliation. Their suffering was rewarded with a form of freedom that was not as generous as that accorded to others who had confessed. The ailing men were dispatched to monasteries to perform further penance for their crimes.

Following the London show trials and absolutions, a public confession by other Templars took place outside the city of York's cathedral.

Eventually, every Templar in England succumbed to the pain of torture and took the offer of freedom, with the exception of two: the Grand Master, William de la More, who died toward the end of 1312 in solitary confinement at the Tower of London, and Brother Himbert Blanke, the Grand Preceptor of Auvergne in France, who had been imprisoned in England. De la More died proclaiming his innocence and the order's. In a rare display of generosity, King Edward declined to confiscate the Master's personal possessions and ordered them sold to pay off the dead man's debts, which ironically included the cost of his imprisonment, and may explain Edward's atypical lack of avarice.

Blanke's end was especially sad and disgraceful in light of his service in Palestine and his reputation as a warrior. After the fall of Acre, he had remained in the Holy Land and led guerilla-style actions against the victors. The order's elder statesman, and a general who should have ended his days honored like an Eisenhower rather than a Pétain, Blanke instead spent the last five years of his "retirement" in a dungeon in London. Weighed down with a double set of chains and visited by inquisitors who failed to crack the old man's resolve, Blanke died of so-called natural causes.

Despite the use of torture and the ferocious reputation of its indigenous Inquisition, the campaign against the Templars in Tarragona and Aragon in what is modern day Spain failed to extract confessions from members of the order there. The Templars were also vindicated in Portugal and Germany.

The nineteenth-century historian Charles Addison overstated the case when he claimed the Templars only "came to grief" in France and the papal domains, since the fate of the English Temple, although not as grim as its French counterpart, included dissolution, if not annihilation.

The drama and public theatrics continued in France. On October 16, 1311, the Pope himself made the trip to Vienne, near Lyons, for an assembly at which he proclaimed the abolition of the order after a public reading of the accusations and confessions of its members.

What had been intended as a monotonous formality blew up in the Pope's face when he found himself confronted by a rebellion among the French ecclesiastical hierarchy. While the Pope's nephew, an Italian prelate, and the Bishops of Rheims, Sens, and Rouen fell in line behind the Pontiff, the rest of the churchmen demanded that before the dissolution of the order, which included burning the guilty at the stake, those about to die should be allowed to plead their case.

The King and the Pope were enraged by this clerical mutiny, and the Pope immediately dismissed the assembly to prevent further embarrassment. Citing his own authority, which he pointed out required no clerical

imprimatur, the Pope announced that he would pro-
nounce the sentence himself. Before he burned such
once powerful and respected monastics, the Pope
decided to bolster his position by calling a private gathering of French ecclesiastics in early 1312. The closed-
door nature of the assembly would prevent another
embarrassment if the new gathering proved as muti-
nous as the previous one at Vienne. The Pope need not
have worried. He was more successful at this assembly
and managed to coerce several formerly recalcitrant
French cardinals and bishops into ratifying his ordinance to dissolve the order. The Pope's new declaration dissolving the order added the term "in perpetuity"
to the document, which was so intent on eradicating
all vestiges of the Templars that the mere wearing of
its famous mantle with a red cross would lead to
instant excommunication. The garment that Western
Christendom had once worn as a coveted sign of com-
mitment to the rescue of Jerusalem would now send its
wearer straight to hell.

At a second session in Vienne in the spring of 1312,
the Pope and Philip, with three of the King's sons in
attendance, jointly decreed the order's abolition. They
may have feared violent objections to the decree, since
a large force of royal troops flanked the Pope and King
when the proclamation was read out. Unlike previous

moves against the order, no debate or testimony was allowed before the dissolution was announced.

Only one last act remained in the farce that the trials and public punishments of the Templars had become. The international leader of the order, Jacques de Molay, still unrepentant, had to be disposed of. Unlike the relative kindness with which the English leaders were allowed to fade away like old soldiers in prison or monasteries, the fury of the French King demanded a more violent disposition of the main sinner.

By March 1314, the once great de Molay, now in his seventies, had languished in prison for more than seven years. During his incarceration, the harsh conditions of imprisonment and torture had made him confess, but he recanted, then claimed the confession itself was a forgery. In one last desperate gambit to save himself, de Molay called his accusers liars and challenged the churchmen to settle the matter in a venue, unlike trials and dungeons, where his military prowess would give him the upper hand—trial by combat. To no one's surprise, the Pope, the King, and the inquisitors didn't take de Molay up on an offer that would have been suicidal for all of them, except possibly the warrior King.

Instead of in a joust or sword fight, de Molay met his end on a scaffold set up on March 18, 1314, in front of the cathedral of Notre Dame in Paris. The public was invited and turned out to hear the charges against the Templar leader read one more time by the Bishop of Alba.

Also condemned to the stake were three other highborn and well-connected Templars: Guy de Dauphiny, the Grand Preceptor of France and a brother of the Prince of Dauphiny; Hugh de Peralt, the Visitor-General of the Order; and Geoffroi de Charney, the Grand Preceptor of Normandy. They were brought to the place of execution wearing the infamous double chains. Fearing a public uprising, the King had a large contingent of his men accompany the condemned.

Desperate or perhaps guilt-ridden, the Papal Legate begged the convicted men one last time to recant their recantations and confess their crimes. Guy de Dauphiny and Hugh de Peralt had a change of heart as the kindling wood was laid at their feet, and they accepted the legate's offer.

De Molay remained unfazed by the wood piled up around him and, raising his arms draped with chains, made a different kind of confession to the crowd, whom the King now, no doubt, regretted having invited. "I do confess my guilt . . . which consists in having, to my shame and dishonour, suffered myself, through the pain of torture and the fear of death, to give utterance to falsehoods, imputing scandalous sins and iniquities to an illustrious order, which hath nobly served the cause of Christianity. I disdain to seek a wretched and disgraceful existence by engrafting another lie upon the original falsehood." De Molay's speech inspired the remaining condemned Templar, Geoffroi de Charney, the Grand Preceptor of Normandy, to declare his innocence to the crowd.

At this point, fearing their impassioned speeches might cause a riot that would free the two men, the Papal Legate had them hustled off the scaffold and returned to prison. Their reprieve would be short-lived—only a few hours, in fact.

As soon as the King learned of the incident, he flew into a rage. Without bothering to consult his co-conspirators, the Pope and the bishops, he immediately ordered the execution of de Molay and de Charney. This time, however, the public was not invited. Instead of a public spectacle outside Paris' most famous religious landmark, the scaffold was set up on a small island in the middle of the Seine near the King's private garden and the convent of St. Augustine. The manner of the victims' execution reflected the King's anger. Instead of kindling wood that would consume them in a quick blaze, small amounts of charcoal were the principal incendiary used to provide a slow, excruciating death. Joan of Arc suffered a less painful end.

At their end, the two old warriors displayed a stoicism that was praised by eyewitnesses, according to the contemporary chronicler and monk, Guillaume de Nangis, who wrote, "They were seen to be so prepared to sustain the fire with easy mind and will that they brought from all those who saw them much admiration and surprise for the constancy of their death and final denial."

The mythology that followed the violent end of the Templars began almost immediately. Their chief attackers seemed to have been punished for their crimes against the knights. Thirteen months after de Molay's death, his papal persecutor suffered a fatal attack of dysentery. Even after his death, it seemed that the Templars' revenge pursued the Pope, whose corpse caught fire while on display in a church in Carpentras, France. His relatives were also punished. The vast fortune the corrupt Pope left them was stolen by German and Italian *condottieri* from a church where it had been left for safekeeping.

Before his death, the Pope had ordered the Templars' treasure be turned over to their rivals, the Knights Hospitaller, but the transfer never took place and the order's wealth ended up in the hands of the rulers of the countries that persecuted them. The Kings of Castile,

Aragon, and Portugal put a kinder face on their greed and donated the confiscated lands and money to new religious military orders, then named themselves Grand Masters of the organizations. The Kings of Bohemia, Naples, and Sicily did not even bother to hide their seizures with the medieval equivalent of dummy corporations and appropriated the Templars' property outright. The venal descendants of pious philanthropists who had bequeathed their estates to the Templars enjoyed some success in reclaiming their patrimony, as did the Knights Hospitaller, who ended up suing to have some of the Pope's bequest carried out. Although he had enjoyed the rent and other revenues generated by the Templars' estates during their seven years of imprisonment, King Philip had the cheek to sue the Hospitallers for the £200,000 he claimed it had cost to prosecute and imprison the Templars. His son, Louis X, aptly nicknamed Le Hutin (the Stubborn), demanded and got £60,000 from the Hospitallers before turning over the estates he had seized from the order.

The King of France died of unknown causes the same year as his papal ally. His last year saw personal and political traumas. The clergy and nobles revolted against his taxes. The revenge of the Templars did not spare his heirs. Three of his sons' wives were convicted of adultery and two of them were executed.

The superstitious, which was everybody at the time, would have agreed with the medieval chronicler, Monsieur Raynouard, who wrote, "History attests that all those who were foremost in the persecution of the Templars came to an untimely and miserable death."

Edward II, the English King who was kinder to his Templars than his French counterpart, suffered more and died of causes so well known—anally disemboweled with a fire poker by courtiers who objected more to his homosexual lovers than his failures on the field of battle—you can imagine the Victorian Addison blushing when he wrote of Edward's karmic fate, "The misfortunes of Edward the Second, King of England, and his horrible death in Berkeley Castle, are too well known to be further alluded to." Or too unpalatable for the historian's nineteenth-century readers.

Like most of the myths surrounding the Templars, Edward's fate is hard to link directly with that of his victims. The head of the English Temple, William de la More, died in prison in 1312. Edward was murdered fifteen years later. During that time, the revenues generated by Templar monasteries, manors, and farms flowed into the coffers of the Court of the Exchequer, which was the same as the King's purse. Supervision of the estates was left to local clergy and temporal magnates, like the Bishops of Lichfield and Coventry, a Norfolk squire named John de Wilburgham, and thirty-two other guardians. While the leadership of the order was dispossessed, the rank and file and servants were pensioned off and allowed to remain in their monasteries and places of employment.

Even before their dissolution, Edward could not resist helping himself and his favorites to the imprisoned monks' wealth. In January 1312, William de Slengesby, who administered the Templars' manor of Ribbestayn in Yorkshire, was ordered to send the King's constable in the castle of Knaresburgh 100 "quarters" of corn, ten quarters of oats, twenty "fat" oxen, eighty sheep, and two "strong carts" to feed the garrison's castle. The King promised to reimburse the order from his Exchequer at the end of the year, but never did. A month later, Edward did not bother to make a pretense of repayment and granted the Templars' Yorkshire manors of Etton and Cave outright to a royal favorite, the Earl of Athol. The King's grant listed the portable wealth of the manors, down to the serving utensils and chapel reliquaries, and ordered all of it turned over to the Earl.

The Pope was horrified by these land grabs and grants, and issued bulls that were either rejected or ignored. At the Council of Vienne that had served as the site of a Templar trial, the Pope issued a bull on May 16, 1312, ordering the transfer of Templar property to the Knights Hospitaller despite the fact that a final judgement hadn't been made against the orders' leaders. Bulls specifically addressed to the Archbishops of Canterbury and York, ordering them to comply, were not carried out.

On August 21, Edward wrote to the Hospital's chief in England that the Pope's order infringed on royal prerogative and Parliamentary turf. More to the point, the King's letter sent to Hospitaller headquarters at Clerkenwell told the Prior not to attempt seizure of the Templar property "under severe pains and penalties."

In January 1313, Edward made his biggest and most symbolic confiscation, the London Temple itself, which he turned over to another favorite, Aymer de Valence, Earl of Pembroke. In May, he repaid loans from London merchants by handing over Templar manors to his creditors. By year's end, Edward relented after a flurry of papal remonstrances, and he ordered all Templar lands transferred to the Grand Master of the Knights Hospitallers. The recipients of the King's largesse, however, refused to part with their new possessions and bribed judges to rule that the King had no power to dispossess them of his previous gifts. The Pope, now back in Rome, excommunicated the disobedient property holders.

Almost a decade later, the Pope's successor was still involved in the property dispute. In a bull issued in 1322, Pope John XXII reminded the Templar beneficiaries that their disobedience would condemn them to hell. His bull suggested how pervasive greed was when the Pope complained that even the English clergy who received a share of the Templars' wealth refused to turn it over to the Hospitallers.

Finally, in 1324, Pope John convinced the English Parliament to order the transfer of Templar property to the Hospitallers. Parliament may have been galvanized to act after more than a decade of papal jawboning because of what the Pope promised the money would be used for—a new Crusade to rescue the Holy Land. But the holders of Templar property in England, most of whom were powerful magnates, refused to comply with Parliament's orders, arguing that it had no jurisdiction over royal gifts.

Twenty years after the Templars' dissolution, their property in England was still being fought over. In 1334, during the reign of Edward's son, Edward III, Parliament passed another act confirming the transfer to the Hospitallers and ordered local sheriffs to enforce the order in the King's name.

Meanwhile, the lower-ranking Templars, who had escaped punishment, suffered a form of benign neglect.

Despite the official promise of financial support, neither the King nor the favorites who received the order's property contributed the pension of fourpence a day promised the survivors, who were mostly servants. One historian claimed the monks were on the point of starvation, but since this case of arrears had been going on for more than twenty years, it was unlikely the situation was that severe—if so, the victims would not have endured their neglect for so long.

Shedding crocodile tears, Edward III, who had followed his father in expropriating the monks' property, reprimanded the Prior of the Hospitallers at Clerkenwall for failing to provide for the dispossessed Templars. According to Edward's letter to the Prior, the once proud monks were in danger of becoming homeless, and the King ordered the Prior "not suffer them to come to beggary in the streets." The Archbishop of Canterbury also took the Hospitallers and other beneficiaries to task for failing to pay the stipends and wrote, "This inhumanity awakens our compassion, and penetrates us with the most lively grief. We pray and conjure you in kindness to furnish them, for the love of God and for charity, with the means of subsistence." The Archbishop's complaint reeked of hypocrisy since he was also one of the prelates who had been enriched with Templar property and could have paid or supplemented the pensions. Indeed, the Archbishop of York paid for the impoverished monks' upkeep in monasteries under his jurisdiction.

Higher-ranking Templars were too proud or practical to wait for government welfare that took decades to come, if at all. Fearing persecution or worse, many monks assumed secular clothing and blended in with the population. Although they had been criticized for extravagance before their dissolution, once they joined society their love of luxury increased to the point where the Pope condemned their sybaritic lifestyle. The monks abandoned their vows of celibacy and married, which also prompted a reprimand from Rome. In a papal bull sent to the Archbishop of Canterbury, the Pope declared these marriages "unlawful concubinages" and reminded the former monks that although their order had been dissolved and their leader burned at the stake, they were to maintain their "perpetual" vows of chastity and abandon their wives. To make sure they returned to celibacy, the Pope ordered them to take up residence in monasteries.

During their sojourn in the Holy Land, the Templars had adopted the Muslim custom of wearing long beards, which had symbolic and practical significance, distinguishing the faithful from the beardless eunuchs who served as courtiers and bureaucrats throughout the Islamic world. When the Templars returned to

Western Europe after the fall of Acre, the beards returned with them. After the dissolution of the order, they were so stigmatized that anyone wearing a beard was in danger of being executed. Or as the historian Charles Addison overstated the situation, "When the fugitives who had thrown off their habits were hunted out like wild beasts, it appears to have been dangerous for laymen to possess beards of more than a few weeks' growth."

Beards were so dangerous that when Edward II's valet made a solemn oath not to shave until he had made a pilgrimage to a saint's shrine, his appearance put him in such jeopardy that Edward dictated a letter which the valet carried, explaining his hirsute condition and ordering that no one attack him on his journey.

PART THREE

Legend

Centuries after their official end, who and what destroyed the Templars remain problematic among historians. No modern day writers believe the charges of demon worship and most doubt the allegations of homosexual activity, either recreational or sacerdotal. But what prompted the people who killed de Molay and fifty-four of his monks? What were their motives?

In Peter Partner's *The Knights Templar and Their Myth* (1990), the author insists that avarice played second fiddle to the main tune, a sincere religious conviction that the Templars were in league with the devil. "Greed and envy may have influenced the accusers, but in the forum of their own conscience they felt that they fought God's fight against the Devil and his works." Trying to read the minds of people who died more than half a millennium ago is always tricky business, especially minds ruled by superstition that today seems ludicrous at best, and more likely hypocritical.

Was it a coincidence that a financially bankrupt King chose to attack the richest organization in his kingdom on grounds that today seem morally bankrupt and judicially suspect? Philip engaged in a literal witch-hunt that also enriched him in the process. The motive of greed seems inescapable when even royals like the two Edwards of England, predisposed to favor the Templars for past and future services, found it impossible not to loot a vast "natural" resource, undefended and ripe for the picking.

Partner also writes, "The ruin of the Templars probably came from the most fundamental of feudal motives, the King's anger at recalcitrance or imagined disobedience on the part of his vassals." If disobedience fueled Philip's wrath, and his need for an orderly polity prompted his behavior, why didn't he turn his attention on other unruly vassals—for example, his secular magnates who, much more than the Templars, represented kingdoms within a kingdom and ruled their fiefs like autonomous principalities? The grisly fate of Edward II screams the obvious—his nobles rather than his monks needed to be suppressed before they got the chance to commit regicide.

Partner seems unfair when he suggests that although there may have been no blazing fire, there was suspicious smoke when it came to the charges of heresy, devil worship, and homosexuality, despite the fabricated flavor the monotony of so many similar confessions to those charges has: "Perhaps, particularly after the return from the Holy Land which deprived them of the chance of a martyr's death in battle against the infidel, some Templars *strayed into unorthodox ways*. But the evidence of the trials and examinations outside France suggests that if there were such monks engaged in unorthodox ways, they were few in number. And that, though there may have been irregularity, there was no real heresy." In other words, idle hands no longer devoted to holy warfare became the devil's workshop. No other modern day historian buys this generous interpretation of the validity of the charges brought against the Templars, whose real sin in a jealous, concupiscent world seemed nothing more grievous than financial success.

According to legend, Jacques de Molay called out from the stake to Philip and Pope Clement to join him within a year in answering before God for their sins. A little more than a month later, Pope Clement was dead from dysentery. Within the year, Philip died of unknown causes. The apparent fulfillment of the

Grand Master's curse lent credence to the belief in the order's occult powers. Another unproven explanation offered by some historians is that surviving agents of the Templars poisoned the Pope and Philip.

The legend of the Grand Master's curse has been embroidered in the ensuing centuries. Chroniclers claimed that de Molay cursed the entire line of French Kings. One of Philip's successors, Henry II, died during a joust in which an opponent's lance pierced his eye and brain. Henry IV was assassinated by a Protestant zealot. The most famous "victim" of the curse may have been Louis XVI. One legend claimed that a descendant of the Templars leapt onto the scaffold after Louis was beheaded and dipped his hand in the King's blood while shouting, "Jacques de Molay, thou art revenged!" It is testament to the powerful mythmaking the Templars still generated 400 years after their dissolution that such a well-attended event as Louis' execution gave rise to accounts of an incident that no reliable eyewitnesses recorded.

If Philip's motivations were for the most part pecuniary, he failed to achieve his ends completely. A century of luxurious living had domesticated these once fearsome warrior monks, and throughout the country, the Templars submitted without a fight to the King's bailiffs when they showed up at their monasteries with the medieval equivalent of a Brink's truck to haul away the monks' loot.

But possibly forewarned by their network of spies, the Templars managed to disperse most of their portable wealth before the King's henchmen came to confiscate it. Indeed, the royal agents found monasteries that had in large part been abandoned by their members. When Philip's men tried to seize the Templars' powerful fleet at the port of La Rochelle in Southern France, they found the ships had set sail—never to be seen again. Smaller Templar fleets in the south and north of France, Flanders, and Portugal also left port—and sailed into legend. The disappearance of this huge navy into thin air remains one of the great mysteries of the Middle Ages. Also missing from the Templars' strongholds were the documents and records of their far-flung financial empire. Some historians have speculated that the order's possessions may have been carried by the Templars' private fleet from the port of La Rochelle to destinations unknown. In any case, the money and records never resurfaced.

More likely, Philip failed to seize the fabled "treasure of the Templars," because, like the secret riches of the Jews, the monks' wealth had always been more fantasy than reality.

The Templars fared better farther north. Scotland was at war with England at the time of their dissolution, and many English and French Templars sought refuge in Scotland. The Pope had excommunicated the Scottish King, Robert Bruce, in 1306, one year before the papal decree that dissolved the Templars. Already condemned by Rome, Bruce ignored the papacy, and Templar forces reportedly fought alongside the King in 1314 at the Battle of Bannockburn, which guaranteed Scottish independence from England for three more centuries. Contemporary chroniclers maintained that the superior military skills of the Templars tipped the battle in Bruce's favor, since the Scottish King had only 6,000 warriors facing 20,000 Englishmen. According to legend, despite their superior numbers, the English forces fled the field when the Templars seemed to appear out of nowhere, charging from the hidden rear of the regular Scottish troops. The image of the Templars, with their white tunic and red cross, looked as though the ghosts of the long ago Crusades had suddenly materialized to provide miraculous assistance to the outnumbered Scots. Although his troops were actually winning the battle, the English King, Edward II, retreated in terror upon seeing these ghostly apparitions, with his men following the royal lead. Despite many other failings, Edward's defeat at Bannockburn was the last straw that prompted his nobles to kill him.

Legend, but no contemporary records, claim that the order continued to thrive in Scotland for another four centuries. Descendants of the Templars were said to have fought on the side of the Catholic James II in Scotland and Ireland against his Protestant son-in-law, William III.

In Germany, after the dissolution of the order, the Templars simply shaved their beards, put on secular clothes and disappeared into the general population. Others threatened weak German princelings and won acquittal in German courts on charges similar to the ones brought in France. Despite their official innocence, the order was disbanded in Germany, and some Templars joined the Hospitallers and the Teutonic Knights.

In Spain, the Templars also joined other monastic orders. In Portugal, they simply changed their name to the Knights of Christ. Vasco da Gama was one of these latter-day Templars, and his patron, Prince Henry the Navigator, the King's brother, served as Grand Master of the order.

Columbus' ships sailed under the Templars' banner of the red cross on a white background, and he was married to the daughter of a former Portuguese Templar.

Columbus himself may have been a secret member of the outlawed group since he always signed his name with a distinctive triangle that made up part of the old Templar seal.

Despite their official dissolution, the Templars continued to live on in legend and generate conspiracy theories for centuries. The creative fervor with which people believed in the continued existence of the Templars resembles today's conspiracy buffs who insist that the U.S. government is sitting on explosive evidence of extraterrestrial visits to the deserts of the Southwest.

Eventually, the pessimism and cynicism of the failed Crusades reached their logical and philosophical end—nihilism. Depending on one's cultural and historical point of view, the Templar legend had nowhere to go but up or down, transcending its past or degenerating into myth, elegiac fables, tall tales, and even risible whoppers.

But before examining the *outré* stories that grew up around the order, it is important to recognize one serious consequence of the end of the Knights Templars. In a tangential but ineluctable chain, the end of the Crusades was the beginning of the Reformation. The demonstrable and dramatic failure of "Catholic" good acts against bad infidels in the East created a crisis of doubt and disbelief that buttressed Luther's later contention that salvation could be achieved by faith alone and not at the point of a sword, however well-intentioned and well-pointed. One historian said that Luther might just as well have pounded his ninety-five theses into the church door at Wittenberg with the butt of an abandoned Crusader's lance or mace.

Learned opinion about the guilt or innocence of the Templars vacillated over the centuries, reflecting more the *zeitgeist* than the available facts in the case. While the Templars' contemporaries beyond the control of the Papacy and Philip (Dante, Boccaccio, the historian Villani, and the theologian Sant'Antonino) believed the Templars were the victims of royal greed and papal timidity, a century later, papal historians continued to support Clement's actions and referred to the "pernicious blasphemy" of the Templars. While these Roman scholars upheld the decision of their boss's predecessor for obvious reasons, there was no temporal duress in the form of a local king or prince to lead them to what may have been an honestly arrived at opinion. But a century later, in the full flush of the hyperrationalism of the Counter Reformation, papal scholars, no longer beholden to a Pope dead for 200 years, began to question the official party line. The sixteenth-century Dominican friar Chacon echoed Boccaccio and Dante and not only declared the Templars' innocence, but ascribed their downfall to the financial, not spiritual, preoccupations of Philip.

Centuries later, English writers also took a rationalist's view, but still found the Templars guilty—not of the medieval hokum of idol-worship and erotic initiations, but of losing the faith and their way in a manner well known in England at the time. The Templars had stopped living the religious life and become secular sybarites with tonsures. They were justly dissolved by the King for failures of faith and asceticism, not for crimes and abominations against human nature. "For they held no religion, but lived luxuriously. They were destroyed and brought down through ordinance of the King," the British historian Thomas Wright wrote in 1859.

This Victorian interpretation of events paralleled the actions of Henry VIII, who "destroyed and brought down" the wealthy monasteries of his Kingdom, but like Philip before him, greed rather than revulsion toward monastic sybaritism motivated Henry.

Superstition coexisted with rationalism during the Reformation, and one of the sixteenth century's most influential of the texts on magic, De Occulta Philosphia, by the German humanist Henry Cornelius Agrippa of Nettesheim, contained what seems like a throwaway line about the Templars' guilt. However, the charge this time was witchcraft, not blasphemy—a potent totem and the subject of the early 1500s bestseller, the *Malleus Maleficarum*. Agrippa was lukewarm, even doubtful, when he compared the established demonological practices of early Roman heretics to the later Templar rites. In 1531, Agrippa wrote, "It is well known that evil demons can be attracted by bad and profane arts, in the manner in which Psellus relates that the Gnostic magicians used to practice, who used to carry out disgusting and foul abominations, like those formerly used in the rites of Priapus and in the service of the idol called Panor, to whom people used to sacrifice with their private parts bared." This liturgical exhibitionism reminded Agrippa of another group accused of similar abominations, but he repeated the accusation with a caveat that was almost dismissive: "Nor were they [Priapic worshipers] much different, if what we read is truth and not fantasy [*fabula*], from the detestable heresy of the Templars; and similar things are known about the witches and their senile craziness in wandering into offences of this sort."

Despite his own caveat that the Templars' crimes might have been nothing more than heresy, Agrippa did lump them in with the most abominated group of the time, witches. Agrippa's *De Occulta Philosophia* was one of the most widely read texts on magic during the Renaissance, and it gave new life to the Templar legend. Two centuries after they had exited the world stage, the knights reappeared in a bestseller, accused of a practice that dominated the popular imagination—witchcraft.

While Agrippa displayed a scholar's careful examination of the charges against the Templars and peppered his accusations with equivocations, another scholarly work of the time from the University of Paris, *Les Grandes Chroniques de Paris*, regurgitated the 200-year-old libel that the Templars' initiation rites were orgies masquerading as liturgy. Modern day historian Peter Partner takes these "scholarly" accounts with a grain of salt and says much of the Renaissance writing about magical activity verged on the pornographic itself. In the twentieth century, director Cecil B. De Mille performed a similar disingenuous sleight of hand until the Hayes Office clipped his wings: condemning ancient debauchery by dramatizing in lurid detail just how debauched it was.

Agrippa's influential text started a trend that transformed the Templars from idolaters to witches in the popular mind. In the mid-sixteenth century, the French historian Guillaume Paradin published his *Chronicle of Savoy*, which reported Agrippa's hypotheti-

cal innuendo as fact, with plenty of details to back up his "facts." Paradin's *Chronicle* is most notable for the new accusations he leveled against an order no longer able to defend itself and for the lurid details which the Templars' original persecutors might have been too embarrassed to bring up in open court or even behind closed doors.

Paradin ignored the contemporary accounts provided by the trial transcripts and transferred the Templars' initiation rites from the prosaic confines of monasteries to a more magical place, a cave. He also injected women into the equation for the first time, claiming they were present at the initiations. Of all the crimes the allegedly homosexual Templars had committed, heterosexual fornication had never been one of them until Paradin decided to publish his richly embroidered account. Infanticide was another Paradin addition to the list of Templar abominations. The novices of the order were led to a cave, where they were ordered to worship an image (not identified as a cat or the head of Mohammed), covered with human skin, whose most prominent features were two glowing carbuncles in the eye sockets. The human skin was a new touch, adding the *frisson* of cannibalism to the Templars' cabalism. After committing the usual crimes of renouncing Christ, spitting on the crucifix, and other blasphemous

acts, the monks extinguished the lights in the cave. Then, the women and the famously homosexual monks participated in orgies. The orgy accusation was not backed up by any historical records, but they sold chronicles. Paradin added another cannibalistic touch by claiming that the ashes of dead Templars were mixed in a beverage and served as a blasphemous version of sacerdotal wine during Templar services.

The orgies produced children, which the monks used like a ring toss, passing the infant from hand to hand until the child died. Infanticide was the ultimate *bête noire* of pre-Modern Europe, and the charge was often leveled against another maligned minority, the Jews, who according to the widely believed canard, used Christian infants as a source of blood for their secret rituals.

The Templars had a different use for their dead offspring. After roasting the infant on a spit, a salve was made from the corpse and used to anoint their idol. Despite the heterosexual orgies, Paradin also included the original accusation of sodomy in his account.

Citing the *Grandes Chroniques* of France published two decades before his work, Paradin mentioned an act of Templar treachery which was so inflammatory, had it been true it would, without a doubt, have cropped up in the original trials of the Templars 250 years earlier.

Despite their international renown as champions of the Christian cause in the Holy Land, Paradin claimed the Templars had betrayed St. Louis to the Saracens, who captured the French King with the collusion of the monks. Louis had been a captive of the Saracens, but until Paradin's account, no one, not even the obsessive papal inquisitors at King Philip's court, had ever thought up such a preposterous charge.

Paradin's charges of infanticide and heterosexual orgies were new to Europe, but did not originate with the scholar. He just made them famous—or infamous—in the West. Paradin lifted the stories of orgies and infanticide in a cave from the chronicle of an eleventh-century Byzantine theologian and states-man named Psellus, who predated the Templars and was describing the behavior of a group of heretics known as the Bogomils.

A Renaissance scholar immersed in the new classi-cal learning of ancient Rome and Greece, all the rage since the fall of Constantinople had sent scholars from the sacked capital to the West, Paradin compared the Templars' practices to the orgiastic bacchanals of ancient Rome. He introduced the accusation that alco-holism was endemic among the membership and coined the term "to drink like a Templar," an analogy that never made its way into the original trial. The charge no doubt would have been included had there been any truth to it, but it contradicted the abstemious reputation of the monks.

A contemporary of Paradin's puts the "historian's" trumped up accusations against the Templars to shame. In a defense of the Jews that was rare if not unique for the times, the French political philosopher and lawyer Jean Bodin compared the persecution of the Jews to another maligned sect, the Templars. In his *Six Livres de la Republique* (1576), despite the patronage of the King's brother in whose household he served as in-house counsel, Bodin wryly noted that kings had a bad habit of "filling themselves with other men's wealth and blood." Although he was on the payroll of the King's brother, the Duc d'Alencon, Bodin had the courage to accuse the King's ancestor, Philip IV, of persecuting and executing the Templars on "charges that had been fabricated merely to give an excuse for the confiscation of their lands and goods." This was not a new argument. Boccaccio and his fellow apologist poets had made similar charges in verse centuries earlier, but Bodin was the first to place the extermination of the Templars in the larger context of other witch-hunts, in particular his main topic, the persecution of the Jews. Bodin buttressed his arguments by claiming that German scholars had already proven the innocence of the Templars.

Bodin's reliance on German scholarship served his larger argument against Royal oppression. It took a lot of courage to be an independent academic in Renaissance Europe.

Bodin, however, was a man of his age, and despite the influx of new learning from the fallen Constantinople, he was a firm believer in magic. He just didn't believe the Templars practiced it. The scholar had nothing but contempt for the sixteenth-century bestseller, De Occulta Philosophia, and its author, Agrippa, whom he called a "master sorcerer."

As time passed, the rehabilitation of the Templars grew, sometimes originating from unlikely quarters. More than a century after Bodin exonerated the Templars, a Jesuit priest in Flanders, M. Del-Rio, came to the same conclusion as Bodin. Del-Rio's vindication of the knights is more startling than Bodin's, however, because while the French courtier was a scholar and a man of reason, Del-Rio was the author of the widely circulated Disquisitionum Magicarum Libri Sex (1679), a reference manual used by witch-hunters to ferret out practitioners of the black arts. The man who literally wrote the book on witchcraft examined all the evidence and found the Templars innocent!

The evolution of the historical estimation of the Templars didn't end with exoneration. Toward the end

THE ORIGINAL WITCHHUNT: The bankrupt King Philip IV of France solved his financial problems by falsely accusing the Templars of heresy, witchcraft, and homosexual activity. The order was dissolved by the King in 1314, and its last Grand Master, Jacques de Molay, burned at the stake after rejecting an offer by the Pope to confess to crimes he hadn't committed and save himself from the flames.

of the Renaissance and the beginning of the modern era, the monks enjoyed a coda to their story that had the flavor of nostalgia mixed with romanticism. As gunpowder ended the feudal era and made war an even uglier business, there was a certain wistful longing for a less sanguinary time when men fought with lances that pierced the romantic Crusaders' hearts, not ten-pound cannon balls that cleft torso from legs. At the tail end of the Renaissance, in the late sixteenth century, Crusaders in the Holy Land became the heroes of poems by literary geniuses like Ludovico Ariosto, Torquato Tasso, and Edmund Spenser.

Even the vehemently anti-papist court of James I of England harbored defenders of the Temple. Sir George Buc, a scholar and master of the revels for King James, in his *The Third Universitie of England* (1631), praised the warrior monks for their piety and efforts to "make war against all infidels, and to preserve the Holy Sepulchre of Our Lord and blessed Saviour Jesus Christ from spoil and profanation by Turks, Saracens and other barbarous and cruel miscreants." Buc amplified Bodin's opinion of half a century earlier that Philip condemned the Templars for money rather than piety, and dismissed the Pope as the King's puppet in the dissolution of the order. Buc did a semiotic analysis of the Templar seal, which had been used to buttress the original homosexual charges against the order. The seal depicted two knights riding on one horse. The seal was supposed to symbolize the order's poverty—it could only afford one horse for two knights. The close seating arrangement took on a sinister tone when the homoerotic flavor of the initiation rites was brought up during the trials. But to Buc, the seal was a glorious symbol of chivalry that was already antique by his time, the "modern" seventeenth century. The seal, Buc wrote, was "an emblem of love and charity and true Ieroglyph of religious kindness and noble courtesy of soldiers," which reminded Buc of the "noble chivalry of knights of yore."

The crypto and not-so-crypto Catholic courts of Restoration England gave rise to more Templar champions. Elias Ashmole, one of the founders of the Royal Society of London, praised the Templars in his 1672 tract, *Institutions, Laws and Ceremonies of the Most Noble Order of the Garter*, for much the same reasons Buc did half a century earlier, as defenders of the Holy Land, a region which now existed in the West as a fantastical chimera rather than a piece of lost real estate. The Templars and the Hospitallers, Ashmole wrote, were "the principal columns which supported the Kingdom of Jerusalem for a long time; and therefore their valiant encounters with the infidels and forwardness to sacrifice their lives for the honour of God and defence of the Holy Land ought to be had in everlasting remembrance." An ardent Protestant at the equivocal Stuart court, Ashmole blamed the Pope for the Templars' disgrace. They lost their way when they transferred their allegiance from the Patriarch of Jerusalem to the Pope, who repaid their loyalty with betrayal. Despite his anti-papist cast, Ashmole by now reflected the consensus. The only crime the Templars were guilty of was amassing wealth, and Ashmole called them "a noble Order, no less famous for martial achievements in the east, than their wealthy possessions in the west. . . . Which gave occasion to many sober men to judge that their wealth was their greatest crime."

The Templars' reputation, like fine wine, continued to improve through the ages and generated favorable comparisons to other legendary soldiers of the past. By the beginning of the eighteenth century, the Templars were featured in the Roman Jesuit Filippo Buonnani's popular pictorial, *Ordinum Equestrium et Miliarium Catalogus Imaginibus Expositus* (1711). A prototype of the coffee table book, the *Ordinum Equestrium* included lavish illustrations of the Templars wearing not their signature white mantle and red cross, but the armor of an ancient Roman soldier.

Just as the Catholic court of Restoration England used the Templars for political purposes, the French court dominated by Cardinal Richelieu in the first half of the seventeenth century found it necessary to condemn the order and praise Philip to support the government's Gallicanism, which maintained the supremacy of the King over the French Church. Richelieu's chief propagandists were the royal librarians Pierre and Jacque Dupuy, who published a series of tracts collected in *Traitez Concernant l'Histoire de France, Scavoir la Condemnation des Templiers* (1700). Richelieu and his publicists promoted Philip as the first in a line of French monarchs who defined and defended the rights of the crown over the papacy. The first tract, published in 1654, was notable because it contained the first publication of any transcript of the original trials three centuries before. Pierre Dupuy insisted that Philip took action against the Templars for religious reasons alone and dismissed accusations of avarice. The author quoted extensively from the Templars' bitterest contemporary critic, William of Tyre, not the most unbiased of sources. Dupuy's version minimizes Clement's initial attempt to resist Philip. It downplays Philip's avarice by claiming the Pope gave his blessing to the confiscation of Templar property, even though contemporary documents show the Pope fighting to repossess the Templar wealth that secular powers had appropriated in clear opposition to papal orders.

The Dupuys' treatment of the Templars is tainted by their royal and religious patrons, but the tracts are invaluable to historians because despite their Gallican prejudice, they are the first to print the transcript of the Templars' defense, including the allegations of torture by Philip's gaolers. The Dupuys' arguments appeared so unassailable that for half a century after their publication, no scholar attempted to refute them.

In his account of the Babylonian Captivity, Etienne Baluze, a more independent and respected historian of the time, also found the Templars guilty, but absolved Philip of taking an active role in their persecution and extermination. In his 1693 *Vitae Paparum Avenionensium*, Baluze published the bulls Clement promulgated against the Templars. Baluze insisted these offered such convincing proof of the monks' guilt that Philip had no choice other than to abolish the order—which the Dupuys claimed had sunk into depravity a full century before Philip cleaned up the whole mess.

Ironically, the Templars' mystical reputation fared much better in the eighteenth century, despite its labels as the Age of Reason and the Enlightenment. Nostalgia for the gallant but doomed warriors overwhelmed the better sense of an era of rationalism. The Templars were also the beneficiaries of historical revisionism, which made all Church chronicles suspect and the target of major figures of the 1700s like Voltaire and Gibbon. A middle-class fascination with knighthood and the aspirations of wealthy merchants to ascend the social ladder to that position also created a fascination with the real thing (i.e., medieval knights) and generated more proto-coffee table bestsellers which featured illustrations of the warrior orders worthy of illuminated medieval manuscripts. The lavish eight-volume *History of Monastic, Religious and Military Orders* (1714–1719) by the Anglo-French monk Pierre Helyot, singled out the Templars for special praise that had nothing to do with anti-papist historical revisionism and everything to do with nostalgia for a Golden Age that never existed—except in coffee table productions like Helyot's. In 1721, a four-volume history of the warrior monks was published and cited no less than five other contemporary books on the same subject!

Not only was fascination with the extinct order revived in the eighteenth century, but bizarre reincarnations of it also appeared that survive to this day in the form of Freemasonry.

The unofficial date of the founding of the Freemasons is often given as 1736, when a Scottish knight and supporter of Bonnie Prince Charlie, the Catholic pretender to the English throne, gave a speech in France, where he had taken refuge from his English persecutors. The Chevalier (French for knight) Ramsay was of humble origins but had powerful patrons, including Cardinal Fenelon, Louis XV's prime minister, whose secretary and literary executor Ramsay had been. Despite his humble birth, Ramsay had been rewarded with a knighthood in the Order of St. Lazare, a successor to the defunct Crusading orders. Ramsay addressed a new group of French nobles who called themselves Free Masons and claimed mystical origins in the medieval guilds of stone masons. An inveterate social climber who hoped to turn these French nobles into a secular version of the Jesuits with the King of France rather than the Pope as their leader, Ramsay decided to continue the mythologizing of the Masons' roots. He placed them higher up the social ladder than mere stonemasons and connected them to the monastic warriors of the Crusading era. Ramsay believed a more exalted pedigree would appeal to French aristocrats. Although the Chevalier failed to turn these French masons into a royally sanctioned organization, he managed to attract aristocratic members anyway.

The Templars were still the *bêtes noires* of French history in the minds of royalists and defenders of Philip the Fair like Ramsay, so in his speech to prospective members, the Chevalier claimed the Knights Hospitallers were the Masons' historical antecedents. The only problem with Ramsay's creative mythmaking was that the source of his myth, the Hospitallers, were very much alive and operational in their genuine reincarnation as the Knights of Malta, with a geographical base in the middle of the Mediterranean.

As much as the francophile Ramsay loathed them, since they had all been exterminated, the Templars were in no position to deny they were the original Masons. Soon Masonic lodges throughout Europe were claiming the once disgraced order as their spiritual and literal ancestors, with the old Temple of Solomon in Jerusalem, the Templars' original base, as the symbol of the new order of Masons.

The initiation rites with their secret signs had led to some of the most damning accusations against the Templars. Now, Ramsay justified these signs as a way for the medieval monks to identify Saracens who had secreted themselves among the order for the purpose of assassination. A knowledge of the secret signs would separate the true believers from the *Hashishim*. Citing that historical precedent and thus creating a whole new set of problems and accusations, the Masons adopted secret signs to hide their identities from unenlightened boors who tried to crash the party of aristocratic mystics.

While the royalist Ramsay kept the Templars at arm's length, in the middle of the eighteenth century, an unidentified French author published *De la Maconnerie Parmi Les Chretiens* in Germany, a tract which provided a pseudo-historical connection between the Templars and the Masons. The tract quoted a twelfth-century Italian abbot and friend of Richard the Lion-Hearted, Joachim of Flora (Calabria), who maintained that the Templars were the direct recipients of the wisdom of the Essenes, the first-century order of ascetic monks whose Dead Sea Scrolls were, with the possible exception of King Tut's tomb, the most important archaeological find of the twentieth century. The Essenes' traditions, which had magical or supernatural powers, had been passed on to the keepers of the Holy Sepulchre in Jerusalem, who in turn had passed them on to the safekeeping of the Templars. According to the author of this tract of Masonic revisionism, the true wealth of the Templars lay in centuries-old knowledge of secret powers—not in anything as transitory as real estate deeds or gold. In this account, the night before Jacques de Molay was burned at the stake, he sent his nephew, the Count de Beaujeu, to the Parisian mausoleum where all the order's Grand Masters had been interred. The Count was sent to the crypt to retrieve de Molay's shroud, which de Molay would be needing after his execution. But this was a special shroud, whose voluminous folds contained the secrets of the order, the crown of the last King of Jerusalem, a cande-labra belonging to the Jerusalem Temple which had been stolen by the Emperor Titus when he sacked the city, and four golden statues of the Evangelists secreted away from the Church of the Holy Sepulchre before the city fell to the Saracens. The tract also quoted de Molay as informing his noble cousin that two stone pil-lars in the Grand Masters' mausoleum near the choir entrance were hollow and filled with the Templars' fabled treasure.

Like all the other myths of Templar wealth which had caused so much grief to the order, this tract failed to mention what happened to de Molay's shroud and its glittering contents, nor why real-life masons, once they learned of the treasure-filled stone columns, didn't use the tools of their trade to enrich themselves.

About the same time as the publication of the French tract, another fabulist, a self-styled Scottish nobleman who went under the assumed name of George Frederick Johnson, claimed the secret "wisdom" of the order—"wisdom" seeming to have been a more spiritual-sounding euphemism for knowledge of the where-abouts of the Templar loot—had been relayed by de Molay to some surviving Templars, who fled to Scotland with the information and created a new order, The Knights of the Great Lion of the High Order of the

Lords of the Temple. Johnson also anointed himself
Provost General of the new order and claimed to have
firsthand knowledge of de Molay's lucrative "wisdom."

The ersatz aristocrat Johnson epitomized one of the
attractions of the Free Masons, which provided social
climbing on a dizzying scale from commoner to nobility in an age when class held the same importance as
color did before the Civil Rights Movement.

Peter Partner didn't understate the case when he
wrote, "The invention of the Templar myths amounted
to a patent to create new noble titles on a huge scale."
That may have been the real Templar treasure—
instant ennoblement. As Provost General, Johnson
turned hundreds of members of his organization into
knights, with hierarchies within the order that added
panache and status. Lower-ranking knights were
required to show deference to higher-ranked members in elaborate secret rituals, which fascinated the
hierarchical society of the time. During the Seven
Years War in the middle of the century, a German
minister named Samuel Rosa created seventy-two
Templar "Heads" under the command of nine "Knights
of God." Both Rosa and Johnson were not only great
recruiters but also accomplished charlatans, charging
members exorbitant fees for admission to the order,
titles, and banquets. And since their enterprise was

already based on a myth, Rosa and Johnson felt no com-
punction about embroidering the original story to pro-
mote their enterprise. Johnson boasted that members
of his order had assassinated Britain's Admiral Byng,
who was only nominal commander of the nation's
Mediterranean fleet—Johnson claiming to be the real
commander.

The injection of the Templar myth into Freemasonry
had a pernicious effect on the organization and contributed to the negative reputation and controversy that
plagued the society well into the nineteenth century,
when it aroused the same kind of paranoid suspicions as
communism did in the twentieth century.

The Masonic rituals named "three abominables"
were responsible for the death of the Templars' last
Grand Master, Jacques de Molay. These abominables
were King Philip IV, Clement V, and a mythical
Templar renegade called Noffodei, who according to
Johnson but unsubstantiated by trial transcripts, testified against the Templars in France. The Masonic
Templar rituals were some of the worst-kept secrets of
the era. One ritual was said to involve a pledge by high-
ranking members to avenge the death of de Molay
with the assassination of King Philip's descendant, the
King of France. Whether or not this conspiracy was
true, the French secret police believed the story of the

Masons' vendetta and kept an eye on their members, despite their rank as some of the greatest nobles in the country and servants of a King they were supposedly sworn to kill.

The Templar form of Freemasonry proved wildly popular, transcending borders and oceans. The first Masonic lodge in the New World predated the American Revolution by half a decade. The Templar version of Freemasonry competed with the earlier British version and the first Templar lodge was founded in England in 1778. The German Templars, unlike their brothers in other countries, did not provide social advancement and remained the exclusive preserve of aristocratic members. The attraction of German Templarism, since it didn't provide spurious titles to social climbers, derived from its members' fascination with alchemy and occult practices. The German *Junkers* didn't want status; they wanted to turn lead into gold.

The most prominent and effective leader of the Templars in the eighteenth century was the German aristocrat Karl Gottehelf von Hund, who held huge tracts of land in East Saxony. He was a master of organization and recruitment, and probably a delusional paranoiac. He was not one of the mercenary charlatans that other Templar populizers, such as Rosa and Johnson, were, but his motivations were mercenary nonetheless.

The difference was that von Hund believed his delusions about alchemy. His lodges of "Strict Observers" functioned as research facilities for the transmutation of lead and other base metals into gold, as well as experimenting with other scientific superstitions of the era, including nostrums and life-prolonging elixirs. Von Hund did not believe in academic freedom, and one of the conditions of membership was an unquestioning belief in the discoveries and conclusions of the order. A central belief was that von Hund's organization had been founded by "Unknown Superiors." A lodge in Bohemia sent an "elixir of life" to a lodge in Jena, Germany, which in turn sent a sample to the self-proclaimed Grand Master, von Hund. Von Hund passed the vial on to a Templar doctor in Hamburg, who showed commendable scientific sense and refused his Master's order to try the elixir on human patients, recommending animal trials first. Von Hund lost interest in the experiment and moved on to another delusion, which led him to believe he was a confidant of Bonnie Prince Charlie, the Young Pretender. Von Hund claimed he had met the Prince (he never did) and that the Pretender was the secret head of the order von Hund led.

Von Hund was rich in land, not cash, and he had trouble funding his growing order. For a while, he investigated the possibility of suing the descendants of

the Knights Hospitallers, which had inherited the portion of the Templar revenues temporal rulers and ecclesiastics hadn't seized. The Hospitallers' successors, the
Knights of St. John of Malta, resisted von Hund's
claims, and the dotty aristocrat moved on to new preoccupations and obsessions.

At the time, there were three self-proclaimed heirs to
the Templar legacy, Rosa, Johnson, and von Hund. Rosa
challenged Johnson to a magician's "duel," which he lost,
subsequently leaving the order in embarrassment and
disgrace. Despite his bogus aristocratic pedigree, Johnson
enjoyed support among the North German aristocrats
who represented the majority of his branch of the order.
The power of his position was such that von Hund,
despite being an incredible snob about commoners, at
first attempted to ally his organization with Johnson's.
Von Hund's curiosity may have also been piqued by
Johnson's claim that he possessed an unnamed secret,
which enthralled these latter-day Templars and swelled
their ranks and coffers. The rivals agreed to meet in
1764 at the medieval fortress of Altenberga in Thuringia.
The story of their meeting has the elements of an *opera
buffa* except for the unhappy ending.

Johnson appeared at the castle with his "knights" in
full medieval armor. He justified this show of force
against von Hund as a prudent precaution against

attack by one of the order's greatest nemeses, Frederick the Great, on whose territory they met. Johnson's antiquated army and armor would have proved no deterrent to one of the greatest generals of all time, but von Hund was in no position to complain since he showed up with a retinue similarly tarted up in medieval wear.

Johnson may have ameliorated the situation at first by paying elaborate feudal homage to von Hund, who was, after all, a genuine aristocrat and of higher rank than Johnson in the real world. But the paranoid German hadn't come to Altenberga for feudal ceremony. His lodges provided plenty of that back home. Von Hund wanted to learn the nature of Johnson's secret, and when Johnson failed to deliver during a three-day visit, von Hund denounced him as a "trickster" and challenged him to battle. Both sides were equipped for warfare closer to the kind engaged in by modern day "reenacters" of Civil War battles rather than the real thing, but Johnson showed he was not only no aristocrat, but not even a gentlemen—he declined von Hund's offer to fight, instead fleeing with his men.

Von Hund proved a dangerous enemy and a "scientist" who didn't like to be kept in the dark about important secrets. Instead of letting Johnson slip into disgraceful anonymity like Rosa after his failed magic act, von Hund's network of powerful nobles and spies tracked Johnson down, and in pre-*habeas corpus* Germany had the luckless Templar leader held without trial in the Wartburg fortress for a year before his death in 1775. A year later, von Hund followed his tormentor to the grave wearing a costume he had personally designed as the "Provincial Grand Master of the Order."

The exclusionary nature of von Hund's order, which limited membership to aristocrats, created a spiritual vacuum, which was soon to be filled by a German scholar who created both a competing Templar fraternity, and yet another myth to justify its origins as the legitimate heir to the Templar tradition.

An Orientalist who studied at Göttingen University, August Starck of Mecklenburg, Germany, received a teaching position in St. Petersburg after graduation. Despite his commoner origins as the son of a Protestant pastor, Starck managed to be inducted into a Templar lodge, perhaps because his sponsor was a Greek aristocrat, Count Melesino. The Masons, in fact, helped secure his teaching position in the Russian capital, which he left in 1766 to study the mysteries of the Masons in Paris, where he converted to Roman Catholicism. Conversion was common among Masons at the time because they believed priests were repositories of centuries-old Templar lore and would be more likely to reveal this information to co-religionists.

With or without secrets, Starck returned to Germany, where he set up a new order, not of Templar knights, but something called Templar "clerks," which would be open to non-aristocrats. Starck claimed that during the Middle Ages an order of Canons or Clerks of the Temple coexisted with the military branch. As his source for this fantasy, Starck cited a nonexistent passage in a chronicle by, of all people, one of the Templars' most virulent critics, William, Archbishop of Tyre.

In a version of "publish or perish," Starck created a whole new "history" of the Templars, which had the curious effect of confirming some of the worst accusations made against them during their trials—a bizarre enterprise for someone trying to revive the order.

Starck claimed that the Renaissance writer Henry Cornelius Agrippa of Nettesheim had been a member of the clerical branch of the order, another bizarre allegation since Agrippa had written that the original Templars were guilty of witchcraft, while dismissing the other charges of idolatry and blasphemy. Starck ignored Agrippa and repeated the old libel that the monks worshipped the idol Baphomet . . . and incorporated the act into the initiation rite of Starck's new order! Is it any wonder that from the Enlightenment through the nineteenth century, the Masons were feared and hated by the general public, which suspected them of the worst secret behavior?

Starck was attracted to the idol Baphomet because he believed it possessed magical powers, an ironic contention which the original Templars, despite living in a much more superstitious time, would have never maintained. Starck's regimen for the consecration of a new lodge member or Canon was more sacrilegious than anything Philip or Clement's most virulent inquisitors could have fabricated. The head of Baphomet rested on the altar next to the Bible and in front of seven candlesticks, only three of which were lit.

Starck, who later apostatized his Catholic faith and became a Protestant minister, fancied the more baroque ceremonial of Catholicism in contrast to the stark liturgical practices of his original faith, and incorporated a great deal of Catholic ritual into his Temple for the common people. During the consecration and initiation ceremonies, there were readings from the Old and New Testaments, an exorcism with water, and a christening of the new Canon with oil. The rite ended with a practice that would have sent its practitioners to the stake in pre-Enlightenment, witch-hunt crazy Europe. The inductee sealed his admission to the order by touching the idol with the hope of deriving some of its magical powers.

Like any good scholar, Stark provided footnotes. The origin of this liturgical mumbo-jumbo came from documents he had found in a deserted Templar monastery in Auvergne, France, and another monastery in Russia; this was a preposterous claim since the order had never spread that far. The outrageousness of the provenance may have lent it an ironic credibility (i.e., no one would make up something so patently unlikely).

Starck's "scholarship" became so popular, especially since his aristocratic competitors didn't even provide the academic arguments Starck did, that his Canonical organization attracted aristocratic applicants, whom Starck accepted and attracted by emphasizing the order's love of liturgy and costume. The costume designs reflected different ranks in an order originated from the exclusionary practices of earlier, aristocratically controlled Temples. Low-ranking brothers wore a purple cassock reminiscent of a lay Catholic priest. Higher-ranking Canons echoed the glorious couture of the original members with their floor length white robes and the talismanic red cross across their chest. A purple hat or biretta added a more modern, clerical touch.

Starck's Canonical Templarism attracted huge numbers of new members. Despite his specious scholarship, he was neither a charlatan like Rosa and Johnson, nor a gold-obsessed paranoiac like von Hund. Starck seems to have been a serious if misguided scholar who devoted his life to examining and resurrecting an ancient religious order. His research impressed fellow academics, and Starck received teaching positions at the University of Königsberg in Prussia, and later at the University of Mitau in Kurland.

The popularity and power of Starck's position were dramatized at a conference attended by both von Hund's and Starck's Temples at Kohlow, Prussia, in 1772. For face-saving purposes, the aristocrats and the commoners agreed to merge, but von Hund was in effect forced out and retired with an honorary title. He suffered the further humiliation of being made to announce that he, not the mythical "Unknown Superiors" he had created out of whole cloth, was the originator of his aristocratic Temple.

Starck's hegemony didn't survive much longer than von Hund's tenure, and at the same conference at Kohlow in 1772, the aristocratic caste of Starck's organization was underlined by the election of the Duke of Brunswick as "Great Superior of the Order." Losing control of his creation, Starck proved himself an adept survivor and careerist. He left the Templars to the aristocrats and took up a position as chaplain or Court Preacher to the Duke of Meckenburg-Strelitz in Darmstadt. Starck's strict observance of ritual seemed to have left the order along with him, and German Templarism took on a less mystical, superstitious cast.

Even with a royal German duke as "Great Superior," Templarism found itself challenged further north for political and religious reasons.

The new rival outranked the aristocratic von Hund and the royal Duke of Brunswick. The leader of Swedish Templarism was none other than the King of Sweden himself, Gustav III, who founded the Scandinavian offshoot because the devout Protestant ruler believed von Hund's rantings that the Catholic Bonnie Prince Charlie was the secret leader of the German branch. Starck's and many other Protestant Templars' conversion to Catholicism added legitimate anti-papal concerns to Gustav's unwarranted worries about the Jacobite Pretender to the British throne.

With its quackish alchemy, hoary ritual, and errant Stuart princes, Templarism in the Age of Reason seemed like an anachronism in danger of becoming self-parody. From the safety of a sinecure as chaplain to his ducal patron in Darmstadt, the defrocked Templar Starck wrote with unveiled bitterness in his 1782 tract, *Über Die Alten und Neuen Mysterien*, about the grotesque comedy the order had become. "What is the use of Masonry if it is nothing but a continuation of medieval chivalry? If that is so, it becomes a purposeless, laughable institution," wrote the scholar who introduced the veneration of the head of the Prophet into his neo-Templar liturgy:

> A knight in all his panoply was well enough in the dark and barbarous medieval times in which he served some purpose, but in our day he is simply ludicrous. If he goes out in public, he is a figure of masquerade whose appearance draws the children into the streets, and the more gravely he maneuvers his lance, the more they mock him! If anyone plays the knightly role in solitude, he shows himself to be mentally unbalanced. The whole nature of the world has changed, and to connect the old chivalry with Freemasonry is to think in a way which is no longer consonant with our times: it is like sending a Roman legion out into the modern world.

It doesn't take a cynic to notice that Starck had this epiphany about the anachronistic ludicrousness of the order only after control of it had been wrested from him.

Despite Starck's denunciation, the Duke of Brunswick revitalized the order, and it began to attract converts in Italy, Switzerland, and even in France, the country that had done the most to destroy Brunswick's spiritual antecedents. Although von Hund had confessed that the "Unknown Superiors" who founded his branch of Templarism existed only in his imagination, the Duke remained a believer and sent one of his courtiers, Baron Wachter, to Italy in search of the nonexistent founders. Wachter's mission failed, and although he found the Unknown Superiors remained unfindable, his journey had an amusing fringe benefit when he met with Charles Edward Stuart, the Bonnie Prince Founder of von Hund's imagination. The Stuart Pretender flat out denied any prior knowledge of the order, much less being its founder! The Prince's public renunciation helped remove some of the papist taint which still clung to the order since so many of its members had converted to Catholicism, a fashionable trend at the dawn of the nineteenth century's Romantic movement. Wachter's mission had cost his royal patron a fortune, and the Baron may have felt guilty returning to Germany with nothing more than a bonnie denial. So, taking a page from von Hund's and Starck's self-mythologizing texts, Wachter regaled Brunswick with lurid, "eyewitness" tales of Templar initiation rites that summoned demons from hell and would have made the original order's prosecutors blush. Although he had been unable to find them, Wachter claimed he knew the location of von Hund's Unknown Superiors. They lived with seven monks, whom the Baron also neglected to meet, in seven caves excavated under a monastery in Tuscany.

Wachter's "findings" proved too much for the post-Starck, Canonical branch of the Templars, and members put out pamphlets condemning Brunswick's phantasmagoric tales, splitting the union between von Hund's Strict Observers and Starck's Canons, which had been achieved at the Kohlow conference in Prussia in 1772. A powerful entropy created by both cynicism and superstition fragmented the two main branches into even smaller centers of Templarism.

Wachter's wild tales not only failed to convince his patron, but they seemed to have created something of a crisis of faith in the Duke of Brunswick, who sent letters to member lodges seeking reassurance that the Templars were on the right path. The well-meaning Duke must have been disappointed by the unsolicited reply he received from a nonmember, the reactionary political scientist Joseph de Maistre, whose estimation of the original Templars was positively medieval—not surprising coming from a scholar who would later write a treatise defending the Spanish Inquisition. De Maistre wrote the Duke that the loss of the Templars in 1314 had been no loss to the world. "Fanaticism created them; avarice destroyed them; that is all there was to it."

By this point in time, de Maistre's estimate of the Templars did not reflect their rehabilitation by less reactionary historians.

The Duke made one last attempt to save his branch of Templarism, an attempt that ended up destroying it. In 1782, he called a conference at Wilhelmsbad in Northern Germany. It must have been a depressing gathering of some of Europe's bluest blood, and it certainly resulted in a case of the blues for any members hoping the conference would revive rather than destroy the dying organization. Alchemist members failed to present any new "discoveries" at the conference. The Unknown Superiors were not revealed. And the convocation decided it couldn't prove that their version of Templarism, the Strict Observance, had been practiced by their forebears. The participants voted to remove occult practices and all references to the Templar tradition from their rituals. There were practical reasons for repudiating their roots. The Age of Reason, as Dickens later noted, was also the Age of Darkness, and the superstitious, especially on the Far Right, still believed in the moral and diabolical depravity of the medieval order. In separating itself from the originals, the convocation at Wilhelmsbad explained that an association with the suppressed order would be "potentially dangerous in that it might cause mistrust of Masons among the governments; in any case it was out of tune with modern customs and opinions." Freemasonry remained; the Templars passed back into legend and derision.

A splinter group, the Bavarian Illuminati, which survived the abandonment of the Templar tradition at Wilhelmsbad, proved the convocation's fears were correct when the Illuminati's behavior caused their official suppression by the Bavarian government. While the Templar ritual had been officially abandoned, the Illuminati continued to conduct their rituals in secret, which fueled conspiracy theories about what evil practices went on behind these post-Templar doors. But the real reason for their suppression had nothing to do with hokum and everything to do with their espousal of radical politics in a reactionary Europe terrified by the rampaging Jacobinism of the French Revolution.

Seizure of the Illuminati's papers by the Bavarian secret police in 1787 proved that the successor organization had not followed the orders of the Wilhelmsbad agreement, and Templar ritual flourished amid the Illuminati. Their papers revealed that they still adhered to the Strict Observance, which even its originator, the mad von Hund, had repudiated.

From the safety of his chaplaincy in Darmstadt, Starck, the former head of the Canonical Templars, enjoyed the public embarrassment of his aristocratic rivals. A former exponent of the Strict Observance, Starck became its chief critic, satirizing the practice in his novel, *St. Niçaise*.

By now, Starck had evolved from ex-Mason to anti-Mason. Although he had created much of the ersatz medieval ritual that attracted a huge membership, Starck now claimed the liturgical hocus pocus had been a cover for radical politics, which the Templars' successors, the Bavarian Illuminati, did practice. In Starck's self-serving revisionism, the eighteenth-century Templar revival leapt from medieval idol worship to state-of-the-art radicalism with the kind of unbelievable unlikelihood conspiracy buffs love to believe.

Other Masons also acted like rats deserting the Templars' ideological shipwreck. The German publisher and Mason Friedrich Nicolai wrote a pseudo-scholarly tract adding heresy to the charges against the medieval order by claiming they were the heirs to the early Christian heretical movement known as Gnostics. Nicolai relied on linguistics rather than legend to prove his dubious point, maintaining that the Templar idol Baphomet was not a medieval French corruption of Mohammed, which was true. But he erred when he translated Baphomet as a combination of three Greek words—"color," "baptism," and "spirit"—terminology that was part of the Gnostic liturgy. Historian Peter Partner believed the damage done to the Templar Masonic groups by Starck and Nicolai could not be underestimated and reinforced their centuries' old reputation as satanic fellow travelers.

In 1788, a year after the eradication of the Bavarian offshoot, another turncoat Mason and revolutionary, Nicholas de Bonneville, wrote a tract condemning the myth of the Unknown Superiors and denying the existence of the Templar treasure. A Utopian socialist with a colorful, possibly paranoid imagination, de Bonneville accused the Templars of having the most unlikely ally, the Jesuits. Next to the King of France, the papacy had been the Templars' most persistent persecutor, and to suggest that the Pope's personal "army," the Jesuits, were Templar co-conspirators, shows how willing a gullible public was to accept the most ludicrous accusations made against the dwindling membership.

While Starck, Nicolai, and de Bonneville had the veneer of scholarship to support their claims, the Masonic Templars became such subjects of abuse and suspicion that even marginal detractors received a respectful hearing from a public happy to believe the worst about the society. Count Cagliostro, most famous for trying to scam Marie Antoinette into buying a diamond necklace she didn't want, is less known to history for playing a different kind of confidence trick on the Templars. In 1789, Cagliostro was interrogated by the Roman Inquisition as an "expert" on the order and its secret observances. A pathological liar, the witness didn't disappoint the papal prosecutors.

The Count, who was not an aristocrat but one Giuseppe Balsamo of peasant origins, testified that the remnants of the Masonic Templars, including the Bavarian Illuminati, continued to follow the Strict Observance, something no one, not even its founder, von Hund, did any longer. Cagliostro couldn't resist embroidering his sensational testimony and revealed the existence of an even higher echelon of liturgy than the Strict Observance. He called this the "High Observance."

Cagliostro's accusations were breathtaking in scope. The High Observance called for the Templar hierarchy to avenge the death of Jacques de Molay by destroying both the Catholic Church and every royal head in Europe. It has been said that fear of Freemasonry in the eighteenth and nineteenth centuries was the equivalent of "red baiting" in the twentieth, but Freemasonry, as presented by charlatans like Cagliostro and others, was nihilistic, and must have been more terrifying to believers in the established political and religious order than the Communist threat was to bomb-shelter building Americans of the 1950s.

Cagliostro, a sometime practitioner of the new craze of Mesmerism (hypnosis), transfixed his interrogators with tales of a secret trip to a Templar stronghold in Frankfurt-am-Main, where he claimed to have been shown documents that detailed plans to assassinate all the crowned heads of Europe. Signed in blood, the documents began, "We, the Templar Grand Masters . . ." Like repentant ex-Communists two centuries later, Cagliostro named names—those of the alleged assassins who had signed the documents. The Count strained his credibility by identifying figures so prominent that the Roman court didn't dare to move against these alleged assassins. Even so, the beginning of the French Revolution, with its anti-monarchical tendencies, still only a threat in 1789, gave credence to Cagliostro's conspiracy theories about royal murder plots.

While one pamphleteer linked the Templars to the Jesuits, another imaginative writer associated them with a group at the other end of the political spectrum and claimed the Mason membership was filled with Jacobins. During the Reign of Terror, madness flourished in print as much as it did on the scaffold and in kangaroo courts that dispatched aristocratic children to Madame Guillotine. Imprisoned himself during the Terror, a creative pharmacist named Louis Cadet de Gassicourt managed to publish from his cell a full-length book, *Le*

Tombeau de Jacques Molay, that accused the Jacobins (i.e., the fomenters of the Terror like Robespierre, Danton, etc.) of being secret Templars. The execution of Louis XVI was the Jacobin-Templar's final revenge on Louis' ancestor, Philip the Fair, for executing Jacques de Molay. De Gassicourt fancied himself a historian and also accused the Templars of collaborating with the *Hashishim's* Old Man of the Mountain, whom they had in reality expended all their energies trying to destroy. The Templars also led the charge on the Bastille, according to the mad pharmacist, and the Duc de Orleans, the King's cousin, was the secret leader of these Jacobin monks despite the fact that the Jacobins had ordered the Duc's execution. De Gassicourt's book was a bestseller, and its second printing featured a frontispiece that depicted the decapitated body of the Templars' victim, Louis XVI.

At least one Jesuit could not be accused of being a secret member of the order. The Abbé Augustin de Barruel, writing from the safety of England during the Terror, was a Jesuit and like de Gassicourt, an armchair historian. The Templars predated the Crusading era, according to the Abbé, and their original leader was the third-century A.D. heretic Manes, the founder of Manichaeism. Now the Templars had two early Christian heretical roots, Gnosticism and Manichaeism. The

polemicists seemed compelled to demonstrate that the wrong-headedness of the Templars stretched back for centuries. Medieval witchcraft, Satanism, and idolatry were too *au courant* to satisfy these detractors. The Abbé also linked the order to the proto-Protestant heretics, the Cathars, who flourished in the twelfth and thirteenth centuries. Every left-wing movement had a Templar hiding behind it, according to the Abbé, who identified secret members throughout history. So the anti-monarchical Cola di Rienzo of 1348, called the English Cromwell; the Neapolitan revolutionary Masaniello; Henry IV of France's assassins; and all the members of the Committee of Public Safety, including Robespierre and Marat, were members of what seems to have been the largest, most eclectic and enduring organization in the history of mankind.

The Abbé de Barruel claimed the famous gathering at Wilhemsbad in 1782, even though it was organized by the Templars' royal leader, the Duke of Brunswick, was the event where the French Revolution was planned.

The target of de Barruel's polemics, however, was not the memory or reputation of the long-gone Templars, but their modern day heirs, the Masons. Although de Barruel did believe the Templars had Gnostic, Albigensian, and Satanic connections, their guilt was old news and secondary to the more relevant allegation that the Masons claimed these devil-worshipping, proto-Protestant heretics as their philosophical forebears. De Barruel's centuries-spanning accusations anticipated the Communist witch-hunting concept of guilt-by-association. De Barruel revealed secret Masonic initiation rites that sounded like denatured versions of the sacrilegious practices attributed to the medieval order. In the Age of Reason, the Abbé wrote, Masons swore "oaths of vengeance" against the heirs of de Molay's persecutors, the Pope and the French King, and acted out the sentence by decapitating dolls dressed like them.

Although England gave de Barruel, an aristocrat and cleric, refuge from the anti-clerical and anti-aristo-cratic France of the Terror, his readers north of the Channel gave him little credence. From the fog of his opium-eating, Thomas de Quincey had enough clarity to recall reading de Barruel's ravings about a conspiracy that spanned millennia when he was only ten years old, and even then finding them unbelievable. In a survey of covert organizations, de Quincey marveled at the staying power of a fraternity whose connections bordered on the telepathic. "How men, living in distant periods and distant places—men that did not know each other, nay, often had not even heard of each other, nor spoke the same language—could yet be parties to the same treason against a mighty religion towering to the highest heavens, *puzzled* my understanding," de Quincey wrote.

De Barruel would have been horrified to realize it, but he inadvertently popularized Templar and Masonic lore and made it more accessible to the masses. The writings of German Templars like Starck and von Hund were abstruse and almost unreadable. Even a defender of the Masons like de Quincey complained in his translation of a German Masonic tract, "No German has any conception of style. I therefore did [the original author] the favour to wash his dirty face, and make him presentable."

A shabby historian but a brilliant raconteur with the imagination of a Stephen King, de Barruel was a master of style who made the impenetrable mysteries of the Templar-Masons accessible to the public and perpetuated their myth to the present day.

Not all men of letters were detractors. The kangaroo court which sent de Molay to his death provided dramatic fodder and proved irresistible to several German playwrights and poets—unfortunately, they were all mediocrities whose works were as unhonored in their time as they are forgotten in ours. The great German poet Lessing addressed the issue, only to make fun of the modern German Templars with their secret hokum and theatrical costumes. Two serious verse dramas were produced in Germany in the 1790s, including Zacharias Werner's *Die Söhne des Tals* (*The Sons of the Valley*), which managed to make de Molay's trial and death both gory and tedious on stage.

By the end of the eighteenth century's Age of Reason, reason and repression had eliminated German Templarism as efficiently as immolation had the last of the medieval stock. Von Hund and the Duke of Brunswick's convocation at Wilhelmsbad had dissolved their branch, and the reactionary Bavarian government with its paranoid fear of Jacobinism had exterminated its homegrown Illuminati and their tenuous philosophical connection to the radicalism of the French virus across the Rhine.

In France, however, Templarism enjoyed a renaissance, promoted by the apostate Jacobin, Napoleon, who favored the order because it allowed him to keep an eye on its largely aristocratic members and kept them occupied with ritual and costumes and away from harmful pursuits, like restoring the *ancien régime*.

Like their defunct German brothers, the French Templars founded their new order on fabrications, "proved" by pious or cynical forgeries. Two physicians created the French bible of Templarism. One of the forgers was a Doctor Ledru, the family physician of the Duc de Cosse-Brissac before the Revolution. The other was a seminarian, Bernard Raymond Fabre-Palaprat, who may have become a priest during the Revolution, but abandoned his dangerous profession during the Terror for the safer occupation of doctor.

All the latter-day Templars confronted the same problem: How to link the medieval order to their modern day mutations? In 1804, Ledru forged a charter dated ten years after de Molay's death. The alleged author of the document was de Molay's handpicked successor, John-Mark Larmenius (in English, John-Mark of Armenia), who passed on the leadership of the order to Thomas Theobald of Alexandria. For reasons known only to the creative Dr. Ledru, Theobald excommunicated the Scottish branch of the Templars. This branch still enjoyed the protection of their King, who used their military services against his English nemesis. Theobald also condemned the Knights Hospitaller, since they had inherited the leftovers of Templar wealth. Ledru's forgery was encyclopedic, listing every Grand Master from de Molay to the present day, which provided the much sought-after link after so many centuries of apparent nonexistence. The forgery boasted the added flourish of the signatures of every single Grand Master. Ledru was a tireless forger, but not much of a scholar, unlike Bernard Raymond Fabre-Palaprat. The language of Ledru's "1324" charter is eighteenth-century, not medieval, French. Ledru was also no historian or student of current events, since he listed as the most recent Grand Masters of this most Jacobin of orders several Bourbon princes, the enemies and victims of the Jacobin Revolution. Talleyrand said of the Bourbons, "They remembered nothing and they forgot nothing," but they did remember their elaborate names and titles, and Ledru did not. The sloppy forger garbled the Bourbons' complicated titles when he affixed their signatures to his charter.

Ledru was a good enough forger, however, to attract some of France's highest-born personages, despite his problem with Bourbon nomenclature, and they flocked to the new Templar lodge, named the Chevaliers de la Croix (or Knights of the Cross, in honor of the original talismanic red cross on a white mantle). Unlike the paranoid secrecy of their German counterparts, the French Templars reveled in public ceremonial. They may not have had to hide since Napoleon encouraged the anti-monarchical flavor of the new organization, despite the fact that so many members were also members of the *ancien régime*, which considered the Emperor a usurper. In 1808, to commemorate the anniversary of Jacques de Molay's execution, the French Templars held a requiem Mass for the martyred Grand Master at the Church of St. Paul in Paris. The site had special resonance for the new fraternity since it was near the dungeon where the last Grand Master had been incarcerated before his death. The participants wore elaborate medieval costumes which the medieval Templars would not have recognized. The extravagance of their wardrobe, as fictitious as their "charter," reflected the new Romanticism that was sweeping out the fusty old Age of Reason and idolizing everything Gothic, including the Templars, who flourished during the heyday of Gothic architecture.

The new Grand Master, the defrocked Fabre-Palaprat, led the religious service, in the company of a genuine priest, the Abbé Pierre Romains Clouet, the Canon of Notre-Dame and holder of a newly minted Templar title, "Primate." In contrast to the Bavarian government's persecution, Napoleon demonstrated official government approval by loaning the Templars a detachment of soldiers to accompany the procession. Ledru had kept busy. Not only had he forged the elaborate charter which gave birth to the new order, but he or his confederates had managed to unearth "relics" of equally dubious provenance, including de Molay's bones and sword, along with the helmet of the Dauphin d'Auvergne, whom the new Templars wrongly claimed had been burned at the same stake as de Molay.

If dying German Templarism managed to stimulate theatrical productions, the burgeoning movement in Napoleonic France gave rise to even more enthusiastic literary output. A respected scholar but mediocre dramatist, François Raynouard, mounted a verse play, *Les Templiers*, at the Theatre Français in 1805, which capitalized on the new fascination with medievalism in general and the Templars in particular. The melodrama became a huge hit with the Parisian populace except for one important theater-goer, who wrote a review of the play for an audience of one, his chief of secret police. Napoleon hated the play and felt compelled to write about his misgivings in a letter he sent to Fouché. The importance of the production and its theme was underlined by the fact that the Emperor took time out from a battle in Pultusk, Poland, to write about his concerns.

Raynouard presented de Molay as the tragic hero of *Les Templiers*. Napoleon objected and would have preferred his persecutor, Philip the Fair, in the role of hero. Napoleon did not agree with the playwright's thesis that de Molay was innocent and resented the criticisms leveled against the avaricious King of France. Napoleon's objections seem strange without a time frame, since the Templars were the Jacobins' heroes, and Napoleon the heir to the Jacobin French Revolution. But by 1805, the former revolutionary was now a *parvenu* Emperor and sided with his fellow monarch, ignoring the fact that Philip was a collateral ancestor of the royal family he had displaced in becoming Emperor. Napoleon's objections were not only *arriviste* but philosophical and aesthetic. An armchair poet and playwright himself, he believed political tragedy was not caused by political crimes, but by an ineluctable series of events which created disasters over which the players had no control. A modern psychologist would understand the attractiveness of the positive or flip side of this theory, which meant Napoleon's success in battle and diplomacy was also the result of irreversible fate. On a purely aesthetic note, a man responsible for the death of half a million French in the course of his wars found the depiction of de Molay's torture and death at the stake distasteful to watch on stage.

The Templar legacy continued to fascinate Napoleon throughout his reign, despite more pressing concerns. Along with the person of the Pope, Napoleon had also seized the entire papal archives and had them transported to Paris. Legend had it, much like the three letters from the children of Fatima on deposit in the Vatican today, that the papacy was withholding vital information about the Templars, their secret powers and the location of their fabled treasure. Napoleon hoped to unearth the secret of the defunct order among the papal archives.

Although Napoleon hated Raynouard as a playwright, he respected his scholarship, and Raynouard was one of the few academics allowed to sift through the vast Vatican files when they turned up in Paris along with Pope Pius VII in 1810. Raynouard did a thorough job and published previously unknown information about the Templars, but nothing as racy as Napoleon or the other Templar fabulists hoped. New transcripts of their testimony before papal inquisitors tended to exonerate the Templars, and no evidence emerged about their satanic and idolatrous practices. But scholarship was unable to satisfy or dissuade the popular longing that kept the Templars and their Masonic heirs the bogeymen of choice.

As much as Raynouard disappointed his imperial patron as a literary artist and source of new conspiracy theories about the Templars, Raynouard did present a rational, historical portrait of the order. Other so-called scholars preferred to perpetuate and add new material to the mythology that enveloped the order and its heirs.

The idol Baphomet continued to be worshipped by Templar fanciers. In 1818, the Austrian Orientalist, Joseph von Hammer-Purgstall, published a long essay in Latin, *Mysterium Baphometis Revelatum*, in an obscure academic journal, which took Nicolai's assertion that the Templars were latter-day Gnostics and added the medieval accusation that they worshipped the idol Baphomet. More polemicist (and paid lobbyist) than Orientalist, von Hammer-Purgstall ignored Raynouard's trial transcripts and wrote that the Templars had been "convicted by their own monuments as guilty of apostasy, idolatry and impurity, and of being Gnostics." In a book he published a year later, he made the ludicrous claim that the Templars had been in league with their bitter rivals in the Holy Land, the *Hashishim* or Assassins, and linked the contemporary incarnation of the *Hashishim*, the Ismaili sect which survives to this day under the leadership of the Aga Khan, to the Masons. The accusation of paid assassin added another page to Masonic mythology. It was no coincidence that von Hammer-Purgstall was based in Vienna and a paid operative of the arch reactionary von Metternich, who must have found the whiff of Jacobinism that still permeated Mason Templarism terrifying enough to hire bogus academics like von Hammer-Purgstall to engage in scholarly character assassination.

The Viennese scholar earned his honorarium by adding another heretical element to the allegations against the Templars with his claim that the medieval members followed the teachings of the early Christian heretic Ophites. Instead of spitting on the crucifix as the Templars had been accused of doing, the Ophites confined themselves to cursing Jesus' name. These heretics also required their adherents to renounce Christ as their Savior, which von Hammer-Purgstall accused the medieval order and their nineteenth-century heirs of doing as well. There were no primary sources that indicated the Ophites engaged in sexual debauchery, so the scholar "found" or had manufactured vases he dated from the late classical period depicting the Ophites engaged in sexual acts which resembled the alleged initiation rites of the Templars. Despite the millennium that separated them, the two groups were now tied together by counterfeit archaeology.

Metternich's man in Vienna did a great deal of original scholarship. For the first time, the Templars were also accused of the Gnostic practice of phallus-worship, something Philip and Clement would probably have been too embarrassed to concoct and bring up at the original trials and interrogations—even in the secret hearings closed to a public that would have thronged to them for such colorful stuff.

[Half a century later, a respected British scholar of ancient history, Thomas Wright, was taken in by von Hammer-Purgstall's phallic fallacy and in his essay, "A Discourse on the Worship of Priapus and its Connection with the Mystic Theology of the Ancients," he described peasant rites which involved phallus worship as a form of social protest against the ruling class. The antiquarian was accurate about the peasant ritual, which was based on the writings of another respected historian, Michelet, but Wright added that aristocratic secret societies also participated in this form of protest (against whom? themselves?), and cited the Templars as an example of such a society that venerated the simulacrum of the male genitalia.]

While his predecessors were content to prove their theories with forgeries, von Hammer-Purgstall dug up "concrete evidence" in the form of coins, medals, and bits and pieces of monuments he claimed dated from the late classical period, when heresy thrived, to the heyday of the Templars a thousand years later. The scholar produced two Templar coffins which he said had been excavated from an archaeological dig, but these medieval artifacts were decorated with carvings that depicted Gnostic orgies from the second century A.D. The images on the coffins looked suspiciously similar to illustrations published a few years before in von Hammer-Purgstall's tract on the Templars' worship of Baphomet. It has been speculated that the wealthy Duc de Blacas, a reactionary minister in the post-Napoleonic regime of Louis XVIII, paid to have the artifacts fabricated in the occultist workshops that flourished in Europe during the Romantic era with its love of mysticism and superstition. The caskets must have been a prize possession of the anti-Jacobin Duc and further ammunition in the war against the Jacobin-tainted Freemasons.

Von Hammer-Purgstall's most important contribution to Templar lore was to be the first—but not the last—to connect the order to the pursuit of the Holy Grail, creating a whole new fabulary that claimed a Masonic lodge somewhere still possessed the cup Jesus drank from at the Last Supper. The scholar's source was not a historian, but a poet, the medieval Wolfram of Eschenbach, whose epic poem *Parzifal*, besides inspiring Wagner, created the legend that the Knights of the Round Table, including King Arthur himself, were all Templars. In keeping with his anti-Templar bias, this chivalric association required him to blacken the reputation of Camelot, which von Hammer-Purgstall did by quoting another epic about the Round Table, Sir Thomas Malory's *Quest of the Holy Grail*, in which he described the knights as the "hyghe order and mete wych ye have so much desired." Von Hammer-Purgstall decided "mete" was a variant of "meta," a Greek word for "spirit" and referred to the Templar idol, Baphomet. Another reference to "meta" in Eschenbach's *Parzifal* confirmed the scholar's suspicions. For good measure, he also decided that King Arthur's knights, like the rest of their Templar ilk, were Gnostic heretics, and that the Grail was used in Gnostic services. Although von Hammer-Purgstall's fantastic ramblings were published in a dead language in an obscure Orientalist academic journal in Vienna, somehow his association of the Grail with the Templars became publicized and remains one of the most popular myths surrounding the order. His dubious scholarship influenced such diverse figures as Goethe, Schopenhauer, Nietzsche, and even Marx, who found claims of Christian corruption dating back to the earliest days of Christianity irresistible. Northrop Frey and Levi-Strauss found much of value in Von Hammer-Purgstall's contention that modern social and spiritual concepts have mythical cores.

While scholars debated the origin and culpability of the Templars in obscure Latin essays, the gaudy, popular manifestation of Templarism in the nineteenth century thrived for the same reason theater will always be with us. Bernard Raymond Fabre-Palaprat, the Grand Master of the Templar division known as the Chevaliers de la Croix, created an elaborate constitution for his sect, complete with global aspirations and plans to open lodges in Japan, Russia, and the Congo! Fabre-Palaprat had a Jesuitical mindset and the imperiousness of the division's leader, the Pope. He appointed four Lieutenants-General and Grand-Victors, including a powerful member, the Duc de Choiseul, then excommunicated them via a bull when they displeased him. This phase of Templarism resembled a microcosmic Vatican, complete with an anti-Pope. After one too many excommunications, a rival Grand Master, Count Lepeletier d'Aunay, led a schismatic branch of the Chevaliers de la Croix for ten years beginning in 1814.

Unlike von Hund's branch of the previous century, which attracted an international roster of aristocrats, the cranky Fabre-Palaprat's group consisted of a small number of dotty French aristos left over from the *ancien régime*. The Chevaliers did attract two prominent Englishmen, Admiral Sir William Sydney Smith and the Duke of Sussex; the association injected the comic French cast into serious politics for a period during the Napoleonic War, when Smith tried to get French Masons who were British prisoners of war released.

After the war, Smith felt freer to pursue the association and sought to make the fusty Parisian lodge the hub of an international organization rivaling the glory days of Latin Palestine. Unlike his Grand Master, the contentious and ostentatious Fabre-Palaprat, Smith had practical plans for his idealism. The Admiral hoped to wrest British-controlled Malta from the moribund Knights Hospitallers and use it as a revitalized Templar base. But instead of debating early Christian heretical roots and putting on medieval pageants with embarrassing costumes like his predecessors, the Admiral wanted to use Malta as a launching pad to fight the Templars' ancient enemy, Islam, represented in this era by the Barbary pirates. Smith proposed nothing less than a new Crusade, something that had fallen out of fashion centuries before despite half-hearted attempts to revive the Crusading ideal. Once again, these new monks would be fighting the old enemy. Smith was also at the forefront of the British-led abolition movement, and saw the Chevaliers de la Croix as major players in the suppression of the slave trade, a novel concept at the time. On a less idealistic note, besides dispossessing the Knights of St. John of Malta, Smith also hoped to retrieve some of the Templar fortune the Hospitallers had inherited after the suppression of the order. There was some talk of joining the old Hospitallers and the new Templars if the Knights of St. John could be persuaded to join the Freemasons.

Despite its emergence as the only superpower in Europe after Waterloo, Britain remained in crisis mode in much the same way the United States slipped into its involvement in Korea after World War II. Malta was too strategic for policing the Mediterranean to be surrendered to some idealistic admiral with a nostalgia for chivalry and the very modern preoccupation of eradicating slavery.

While Smith was trying to find a modern, relevant role for an ancient order, his eccentric Grand Master was taking it in the opposite direction, back to esoteric arguments about heresy and mystical rites. Fabre-Palaprat based his new philosophy on an old Greek manuscript, the *Levitikon*, which he stumbled upon in a used bookstore. The *Levitikon*, which was undated, purported to be a revisionist Gospel according to St. John, and its contents were so heretical they would have made the Templars' predecessors, Gnostics and Ophites, blush. But the new Templar Grand Master was not so squeamish and embraced the *Levitikon*, which he made the centerpiece of the Chevaliers de la Croix. The new Templar bible denied not only Christ's miracles, but his Resurrection! Instead, its Jesus was a student of ancient Egyptian mysteries in which God (not Jesus) was a disembodied intellect whose knowledge was transmitted from Jesus to the author of St. John's Gospel, then to the Patriarch of Jerusalem, who passed it on to the Templar's first Grand Master, Hugues de Payen, when he arrived in 1118. Successive Grand Masters continued the tradition, even after the order's dissolution, although Fabre-Palaprat failed to explain how this was accomplished with no Grand Master to receive the information. All members, including non-clerics, had the power to forgive sins and could convey this power to new members.

In 1828, Fabre-Palaprat organized—if "organized" is the correct word—his philosophy around the terms of the High Initiation, the Holy Church of Christ, and the Church of Primitive Christians. The new order, called Johannite Templarism because it was based on the Gospel of St. John, represented a secular religion. Fabre-Palaprat's timing was not good since the reactionary Bourbon monarch frowned on anything resembling the National Church of the French Revolution (i.e., anything outside Roman-controlled Catholicism). It was no coincidence that Fabre-Palaprat postponed publishing his order's bible, *Levitikon, ou Exposé des Principes Fondamentaux de la Doctrine des Chretiens Catholique Primitifs*, until 1831, a year after the liberal Orleanist regime came to power.

Fabre-Palaprat decided his new organization, despite its secular flavor, needed a Pope of sorts and chose a radical priest, Ferdinand Chatel, founder of the French Catholic Church, which though French, was anything but Catholic. Chatel's mix of Protestantism and Gallicanism rejected the authority of the Papacy, denounced the Latin Mass, and anticipated Vatican II by more than a century by calling for a liturgy in his native tongue. Chatel also spurned priestly celibacy and private confession and demanded a Presbyterian-like election of Bishops by church members, not the Pope. The clergyman found the principles of the *Levitikon* meshed with his and asked a willing Fabre-Palaprat to consecrate him "Primate of the Gauls," the religious leader of the Primitive Church—which was another name for Fabre-Palaprat's Johannite Templarism.

For some reason, Chatel's church and Fabre-Palaprat's had separate but nearby headquarters. Chatel set up shop in a converted store in Montmartre and perpetuated the Templar love for the overwrought, decorating the shop with black drapes borrowed from an undertaker, a bust of the tolerant King Louis-Philippe, a tri-color flag which underlined the anti-clerical, Gallican leanings of the new church, and a poster with the names of the three men Chatel considered the most important figures in human history: Confucius; Parmentier, who introduced the potato to France; and an obscure banker and supporter of Louis-Philippe named Lafitte.

Close by in a former wineshop, Fabre-Palaprat launched his storefront church in the Parisian neighborhood of the Cour des Miracles near the Porte St.-Denis.

Like the German Templars of the previous century, Fabre-Palaprat intuited how to boost membership by appealing to the snobbery and parvenu obsessions which plagued the illegitimate Orleanist monarchy, which had overthrown its cousins, the Bourbons. The Grand Master loved to create ever grander titles. The redecorated wineshop was renamed the Apostolic Court of the Temple and all announcements from then on bore that impressive title on the organization's stationery. The membership reached into the highest level of government, stopping just short of the King himself. In 1831, Jean-Marie Ragon, an official in the Interior Ministry and a member of the Johannite Temple, changed his name to Count Jean-Marie de Venise and received the title of Primatial Vicar of the French Catholic Church. A prominent publisher, Guyot, edited the order's "newsletter," the *Manuel des Chevaliers de l'Ordre du Temple*. Most of the members were middle class with aspirations of ascending into the aristocracy. Titles the monarchy failed to bestow, Fabre-Palaprat and his "Pope" Chatel were happy to supply.

Like a microcosm of the centuries-old battles of Caesaropapism, the Grand Master and his Primate began feuding, and Chatel was expelled from the order. The split was so venomous that Fabre-Palaprat brought Chatel up on heresy charges. At the trial, the Primate, who declined to attend, was represented by a rag doll.

Bickering over dogma continued along class lines— or maybe the real aristocrats in the order resented the assumed titles of the bourgeois members. The Duc de Choiseul precipitated a schism, based on his preference for the old chivalric idealism of the Neo-Templars as opposed to Fabre-Palaprat's reworking of the Gospel of St. John, and the Duc led a new generation of French émigrés from the fold.

Fabre-Palaprat managed to preserve the aristocratic veneer of his church by persuading the revered Admiral Sir William Sydney Smith to join his group despite Smith's preference for a chivalric interpretation of the Templar legacy, which was closer to the thinking of his fellow aristocrat, the Duc de Choiseul.

The divisive Fabre-Palaprat died in 1838, and Smith, elected the new Grand Master, reunited the Johannite order with the schismatic Duc de Choiseul's. The reunion failed to revive the movement, which despite great costumes, suffered from its obscure religious preoccupations, and the order dissolved itself by the early 1840s.

While membership first dwindled, then evaporated, the Templars lived on in the nineteenth century in the imagination of major literary figures. While their German champions were minor playwrights in the eighteenth century, in the nineteenth two of the greatest writers of the age found the Templars a source of inspiration for more than one work.

Balzac, the French Dickens and student, if not member, of Freemasonry, in his 1836 novel, *Etudes Philosophique sur Catherine de Medicis*, featured a fictionalized version of Fabre-Palaprat, who accomplishes something the real social-climbing Grand Master never would have dreamt of: an audience with King Charles X and his mistress, during which he lectures his royal listener on the mysteries his order has inherited from its medieval founders. The novel's Grand Master, Lorenzo Ruggieri, demonstrates an eloquence surpassing the dim bulb Fabre-Palaprat and demonstrates the author's keen knowledge of the Templar past and its contemporary variations. With some impertinence, Ruggieri tells the King that although his ancestor, Philip the Fair, burned the Templars' bodies, he was unable to destroy their secret knowledge, which has been transmitted through the ages to the present day. The novel has a Messianic flavor, as Balzac's hero predicts the building of a new Temple, at which time the order will return to full glory. Balzac's work, however, is a comic novel, and after his audience with Charles, Ruggieri confides to a fellow member of the order that he has just perpetrated a giant hoax on his credulous King. But in *Louis Lambert*, Balzac's account of the Templars, the medieval order receives a heroic treatment.

The most famous medievalist of the century, Sir Walter Scott, could not avoid mention of the order, since so many of his novels are set in that era, but his Templars are sinister, not the comic or heroic figures of Balzac's fiction. In *Ivanhoe*, the Grand Master is a bigot desperate to prove his order free of the taint of heresy by accusing the Jewish heroine of the charge. Two other Templars in *Ivanhoe* do not follow their monastic vows, and a third is amoral, verging on atheistic.

The Grand Master and his fellow monks come off even worse in Scott's *The Talisman*, with the leader described as "at the head of that singular body, to whom their order was everything and their individuality nothing—seeking the advancement of its power, even at the hazard of that very religion which the fraternity were originally associated to protect—accused of heresy and witchcraft, although by their character Christian priests—suspected of secret league with the Soldan [Sultan], though by oath devoted to the protection of the Holy Temple, or its recovery—the whole order, and the whole personal character of its commander, or Grand Master, was a riddle, at the exposition of which most men shuddered."

Unlike their vociferous eighteenth-century critics, Scott was operating out of literary necessity—he needed a mustache-twirling villain for the sake of a good story—rather than historical conviction. But that didn't stop the Templar's biggest baiter, von Hammer-Purgstall, from quoting *Ivanhoe* in his own *The Mystery of Baphomet Revealed* as though it were a primary historical source rather than a nineteenth-century romance.

The French travel writer, Gerard de Nerval, in his 1851 *Voyage en Orient*, which was a largely fictionalized account of the author's time in the East, presented the Templars as a synthesis of Islam and Christianity, and asserted that their hybrid faith lived on to the present day in the Christian Arab Druze of Syria, whom he described as the "Freemasons of the East." The Druze's society was a secret one and members, Nerval claimed, recognized one another by showing a miniature figure of the idol Baphomet. Unlike Balzac's charlatan and *Ivanhoe*'s Grand Guignol Master, the Templars in Nerval's account represented a healthy counterweight to a corrupt papacy and monarchy, which unlike his fanciful tales of the Druze, was closer to the historical consensus. De Nerval overstated the case, however, when he interpreted the Templars' anti-clericalism as proto-radicalism and the muse of the revolutions that swept Europe in 1848, three years before he wrote his travelogue.

Despite their different and contradictory presentations of the Templars, Balzac, Scott, and de Nerval represented an important new way of looking at the old order by taking the discussion of their past and present out of the realm of inaccessible pseudo-scholarly diatribes about Unknown Superiors and Gnostic mysteries and popularizing Templarism and Freemasonry in fiction and travel writing.

Scholars refused to surrender the topic to the public and continued to weave fanciful and unscholarly tales about misbehaving Templars. The French historian Jules Michelet was as rabid as von Hammer-Purgstall in his examination of the order and just as ahistorical. Michelet edited and published a transcript of the Templar trials, which should have made him more favorably inclined toward the Templars, since the testimony is replete with evidence of confessions under torture while the verdicts reek of judicial murder. Yet Michelet believed them guilty of sodomy and found their rejection of an auxiliary branch of females as nuns—rather than an antidote to the concubinage that was endemic to medieval monasticism—an unforgivable prohibition since Michelet was a proto-feminist and a fan of the early Ibsen and Shaw.

While apologists for the Templars felt the monotonous sameness of the monks' confessions suggested coercion, Michelet believed them genuine because there were small differences in every confession. He theorized that the alleged spitting on the crucifix and exposing bodily parts during their initiation rites had a sacerdotal origin—a pious reenactment of Peter's renunciation of Jesus after His arrest in the Garden of Gethsemane. Michelet believed the Templars' persecutors embroidered the genuine pious rite until it became the sacrilegious and pornographic ritual that horrified and delighted the spectators in medieval churches and courtrooms.

The liberal Michelet also considered the order's elitism repugnant. But worst of all, as a rationalist rather than a superstitious mystic, he found the Templars guilty of a different kind of idolatry—not as the worshippers of a cat's head but as worshippers of the order itself. The members, Michelet wrote, considered themselves "living Temples." He called this egotism "satanic," although not in the literal sense, while literally believing the trials' accounts of sacrilegious and obscene practices, whose homosexual flavor tied in with the order's misogyny that Michelet found so objectionable.

Michelet's mixed verdict on the Templars—sodomites, misogynists, dupes, and egomaniacs, but not idolaters or witches—became the gold standard for legitimate historians for the rest of the century.

[In one last swipe at the order, an aged, perhaps senile von Hammer-Purgstall came out of retirement in 1854 after reading Michelet's transcripts of the trials and claimed they proved the order's guilt. The transcripts' mention of the Templar reverence for John the Baptist allowed the author, who was a better linguist than historian, to use his language skills to reinforce the accusations of sodomy when he claimed the transcripts' reference to "Janbetif" (John the Baptist) was Arabic slang for "anus."]

Michelet was a liberal and a historian, but not a politician. Politicians who were not historians found other uses for the Templar legend that served their political philosophy rather than history. In 1832, the Italian radical and early proponent of the Italian Risorgimento, Gabriele Rossetti, who would be eclipsed by his son Dante's poetic movement, published from the safety of exile in London a tract, *Sullo Spirito Antipapale che Produsse la Riforma*, which used the Templars' legacy to attack his most despised impediment to the Risorgimento, the papacy. A polemicist rather than a historian, Rossetti ignored the inconvenient fact that the Templars were the Middle Ages' Jesuits and their original charter had the papal imprimatur and encouragement to participate in the Crusades. Rossetti invented an association between the Templars and the heretical Cathars. In his tract, both groups contributed to the philosophical underpinnings that led to the Protestant Reformation. At least the Italian revolutionary was correct about the Cathars and the Reformation, but his assessment of the Templars was as loopy as it was antithetical to Templar critics like de Barruel and von Hammer-Purgstall.

In a second book, which his children blocked publication of because they feared its anti-religious fervor would cost him his teaching position at a British public school, Rossetti declared that the Templars were not only allied with the Cathars, but full-fledged members of the heretical group. Despite his radical politics, Rossetti was a romantic with the love of all things Gothic, which infused the Romantic era. So, the historian-polemicist wrote that the Templars were original members of King Arthur's Round Table, which would predate their recorded origin at the beginning of the twelfth century when Hugues de Payen showed up at King Baldwin's beleaguered fortress in Jerusalem.

The mid-nineteenth-century politician Eugene Aroux adopted Rossetti's linkage of the Cathars and Templars and wrote in *Les Mysteres de la Chevalerie et de l'Amour Platonique au Moyen Age* that before the Inquisition and the Crusades wiped out the Cathars, they passed on their mysteries to the Templars, who

survived their own extermination in successor societies of Freemasons, etc.

While Rossetti and Aroux could only speculate on
the Cathar–Templar connection, a famous forgery in
1877 "proved" the link when a German Mason, J.F.L.T.
Merzdorf, produced manuscripts which described
Templar doctrine dating from the thirteenth century.
The contents of the forgeries suggested Merzdorf was
familiar with the writings of de Nerval, Aroux, and
Michelet, because the knowledgeable forger incorporated many of their theories in his counterfeit artifact.
Although he was a charlatan, Merzdorf was also a thorough researcher, a claim that could not be made for
some of the more sincere Templar scholar-fabulists.

The forged manuscripts read like a Cathar bible,
except they purported to list Templar beliefs, which
included the Cathar's Manichaean heresy of a world
divided between good and evil. Borrowing from
Aroux's transcripts of the Templar trials, Merzdorf's text
claimed that the initiation ceremony included kissing
the genitals, but the forger mistranslated Aroux's
account and had the novice receive the kiss rather than
give it, as the original transcript said. From de Nerval,
Merzdorf injected the Templar alliance with the Syrian
Druze. The worship of Baphomet, which could have
come from any number of texts, also appeared in

Merzdorf's literary hoax, along with an original touch that claimed the opening verse of the Koran was read at the start of the initiation ceremony. By this point in history, induction into the order had become such an encyclopedia of heresies and horrors, it would have taken the busy monks weeks to perform them all.

Merzdorf's forgeries were literary, not liturgical, although they were filled with liturgical references. The fictitious creations of Nicolai and Starck et al. had been perpetuated to provide ritual for their gatherings. Merzdorf was neither a Mason nor religious. He wanted to produce a bestseller, which he did.

The Templars' history and mythology seemed to be a Rorschach test that revealed more about those who studied the order rather than the subject of their study. A cynosure that endured for centuries, these flexible monks could be embraced by radicals and reactionaries, the devout and atheists. Scholars and mythologists at opposite ends of the political spectrum at times shared the same views. Radicals interpreted the Templars as proto-Protestants and Fifth Columnists within the Catholic Church, which the conservatives also believed, but they condemned this role, while the radicals embraced the Templars as their own. In the 1890s, an oxymoronic amalgam of anti-clerical conservative romantics under the leadership of the English writer Bulwer Lytton formulated a utopian philosophy that called for the end of democracy, which it found decadent. Its place would be taken by an enlightened oligarchy of aristocrats. They used Templar doctrine, including forgeries, as the foundation for their movement.

As enshrouded in myth as it was by now, it is not surprising that Templarism was embraced by a more suitable group, folklorists, who put a new spin on a mythology that seemed incapable of further mutations.

While scholars didn't go any further back than the early Christian era in locating the Templars' roots, folklorists antedated them to pre-Christian times. The British folklorist Alfred Nutt, in *The Legends of the Holy Grail* (1902), repeated the earlier belief that King Arthur's knights were Templars, but insisted they were also Celtic priests who predated Christianity. Since the knights existed before the Last Supper, it remained unexplained whose sacred lips had drunk from the much sought after wine goblet or Grail.

Nutt's position was accepted and embroidered by his contemporary, a member of the Folklore Society named Jessie L. Weston, who managed, in *The Quest of the Holy Grail*, to link the pre-Christian Knights of the Round Table to the Gnostic heretics of the fourth century, whose persecuted survivors lived long enough to pass on their secret knowledge to the medieval

Templars. Whatever this knowledge was, which Ms. Weston declined to reveal, it was so threatening to Catholic dogma that the Templars' possession of it pre-ordained their destruction, according to her thesis. What this claim lacks in credibility, it more than makes up for in originality. For centuries, the Templars had been portrayed as victims of greed—theirs or the King of France's, depending on one's reading of history. This new folklorist view held that knowledge, not wealth, sealed their fate.

Fascination with secret societies peaked at the end of the nineteenth century, and prim folklorists like Ms. Weston with her unrevealed Templar secrets were followed by a *fin de siècle* decadence that was only too happy to get into the details of an order which by now had been accused of everything from urinating on Jesus to espousing the ideals of the French Revolution centuries before the event, from being pre-Christian Celtic priests to cat-worshipping Satanists.

A German journalist, occultist, and occasional socialist, Theodor Reuss, created an Order of Oriental Templars, which he used as a means of attracting dues-paying members. Reuss claimed the medieval order had been Satanists. After he failed to make much money in Germany, he relocated to Britain in 1906 with a new title, Sovereign Grand Master of the Order of the Temple of the Orient. Reuss insisted he had proof that his new organization had direct links to the medieval originals, but the information, with its whiff of Satanism, was too inflammatory to have been recorded by the Templars. All Reuss could provide was an oral history, which he was happy to relate, despite its incendiary nature. Besides Satanism, Reuss' rites revolved around phallus worship and genital contact. Reuss made the ancient canard against the Templars real. Six years after Reuss' appearance in England, a more sinister figure took over the order. A British stage magician, Aleister Crowley, styled himself The Most Holy, Most Illustrious, Most Illuminated and Most Puissant Baphomet, X, Rex Summus Sanctissimus, Past Grand Master of the United States of America, Grand Master of Ireland, Iona, etc. Besides the grandiosity of his titles, they place Satanism and idol-worship at the head of the organization's beliefs, with Crowley assuming the name of the cat-idol Baphomet. According to a book published half a century later, The Magical Dilemma of Victor Neuburg, ritual sodomization was part of this order's induction ceremony, something even the most vociferous critics of the Templars never accused them of. One of the victims of this practice was the Victor Neuburg of the title, whose "dilemma" seemed more nightmarish than magical.

Like attracted like. One of Crowley's disciples, Major General J. F. C. Fuller, became a member of the British Union of Fascists in the 1930s.

France's right wing also embraced the Templar legacy. In the 1880s, the conservative mystic Alexandre Saint-Yves d'Alveydre created a new legend which tied in with the popular conspiracy theories of the time. In this new mythology, the Templars were magicians with occult powers which they used to become the real, albeit secret, rulers of Europe during the Middle Ages—a bizarre claim, since the chief of these omnipotent monks ended up as faggot fodder. Like so many other Templar fabulists, Saint-Yves d'Alveydre was a self-made man, and claimed the Pope had granted him his aristocratic title. He lent his imagination to conjuring an all-powerful and ubiquitous group of monks who also ruled in Jerusalem, Africa, and even the spiritual capital of their arch enemy, Mecca! The author's history was as murky as his papal title. Despite their conservatism, the medieval Templars had also formed a proto-Estates General of King, clergy, nobility, and commoners, which was revived just in time to kick off the French Revolution. Saint-Yves d'Alveydre encapsulated his wacky historiography in a book ironically titled, *Le France Vraie* (*The True France*)(1887). Charles de Gaulle, another eccentric conservative, was said to be a fan.

If the leader of the Free French followed Saint-Yves d'Alveydre's writing, he had to keep his enthusiasm to himself because a group of Masons called synarchists were said to be prominent members of the collaborationist Vichy regime. The Masonic offshoot dated back to the 1920s, when its leaders, among them major politicians, businessmen, and scientists, signed the Synarchist Revolutionary Pact of 1922, which was a blueprint for seizing power in a French-style *Putsch*. The coup never took place, and the Vichy regime, with the enthusiastic support of the German occupiers, tried to stamp out the synarchist form of Masonry, despite the fact that a top Vichy official, Pierre Pucheu, led the secret organization.

The synarchists, however, seem to be yet another Templar fantasy, part of a smear campaign against the Vichy government generated either by the Free French prior to liberation or by a Fifth Column of liberals within the Vichy regime.

While the writings of Saint-Yves d'Alveydre failed to create a political movement, he did serve as the muse for fabulists who continued to be obsessed with the Templar legacy into the twentieth century. The Symbolist poet Victor-Emile Michelet incorporated Saint-Yves d'Alveydre's theories into his fanciful *Le Secret de la Chevalerie* (1930), which continued the fascination with the idol Baphomet and the claim that the Templars originated the Estates General of France. Michelet was more poetic fabulist than historian, and he insisted that the medieval Hanseatic port cities were ruled by Druids. This, however, did not stop the next generation of writers from accepting his flights of fantasy as literal accounts of the past.

Working from Saint-Yves d'Alveydre's text, Louis Charpentier in his 1967 "history," *Les Mysteres Templiers*, wrote that Saint Bernard took time out from writing the Templars' charter to send the Knights to Jerusalem to recover the Ark of the Covenant, which was buried beneath their headquarters in the Temple of Solomon. The mission sounds like a sacrilegious theft from the Christian ruler of the city. Charpentier's Templars were the architects of Europe's Gothic cathedrals, which they financed with their famous knowledge of alchemy and with additional silver imported from the Americas three centuries before Columbus. The treasure was dropped at La Rochelle and according to accounts written in the 1960s and 1970s, the loot lies buried in either Gisor or Tomar, France. Television documentaries have explored these claims without blushing.

David Hatcher Childress, a fringe historian who might find more appropriate employment as a novelist, credits the Templars with discovering the New World a century before another alleged Templar, Christopher Columbus, did. In his long introduction to the Victorian chronicle, *The History of the Knights Templars* by Charles G. Addison, Childress claims Prince Henry Sinclair, ruler of the Orkney Islands north of Great Britain, was Grand Master of the order in 1398 when he hired the famous explorer and mapmaker Nicolo Zeno to sail with him from his island home to what is today Nova Scotia. (A century later, Columbus used Zeno's maps to guide him to the New World, according to Childress.) Like an early Pilgrim, the Prince sought refuge for the outlawed Templars in an unsettled land. Henry brought with him 300 Templar colonists and built a castle to house them in Nova Scotia. Childress fails to reveal the fate of the settlers or their Canadian "Roanoke colony." After spending the winter in Nova Scotia, Prince Henry's fleet, which was financed by the long-missing Templar treasure no one else has been able to find, sailed up and down the Eastern seaboard of North America. A likeness of Sir James Gunn, one of the Prince's friends and a member of the expedition, is carved on a rock-face at Westford, Massachusetts, according to Childress.

In 1992, a descendent of the Prince, Andrew Sinclair, published a book, *The Sword and the Grail*, which purported to prove that his princely ancestor predated Columbus' voyages of discovery by almost a century.

Another quack historian, Michael Bradley, claims to have found the final resting place of the Templars' fabled treasure, also located in Nova Scotia. Bradley describes a manmade shaft 100 feet deep and criss-crossed with access tunnels on Oak Island in the center of the province. Adventurers have allegedly spent millions of dollars trying to excavate the bottom of the shaft, which is under water and nicknamed "The Money Pit," since it is supposedly the final resting place of the Templar treasure. So far, the Discovery Channel has failed to visit the place, although the Fox Network may be interested.

Legitimate historians say the shaft was constructed by seventeenth-century pirates who hid their loot there, but Sinclair and Michael Bradley in *Holy Grail across the Atlantic* (1988) both insist the shaft was the work of Prince Henry and his persecuted pilgrims 200 years before English pirates made use of the large hole in the ground. In addition to the Templar treasure, the Money Pit contains documents listing the descendants of the Old Testament King David and Jesus, which shows they were both related to the extinct Merovingian line of French Kings. These fabulists also suspect that the rather crowded Money Pit harbors not only the Holy Grail, but also another alleged Templar treasure excavated during their years in Jerusalem, the Ark of the Covenant.

The fates of other Templars do not have such outlandish tales associated with them and have been amply documented by mainstream historians. In 1522, the Templars' Prussian branch, the Teutonic Knights, secularized themselves, repudiated Rome, and supported Martin Luther. The former champions of the Pope and his representatives in the Holy Land became Protestants—their ultimate revenge, perhaps, against the corrupt puppet Pope, Clement V.

Some Templar rites, especially in Scotland, where the order was never suppressed, live on in the secret ceremonies of their reputed heirs, the Freemasons, according to some students of the organization.

Since many of the Founding Fathers of our country were Freemasons, fringe historians claim the United States owes its existence to the versatile order of warrior monks, who couldn't save themselves but managed to save the American colonies from British oppression. Vestigial elements of the Templars continue to this day in such fraternal business organizations as the Masonic Lodge, the Shriners, and the Knights of Columbus. The Templars' heirs, however, have not inherited the Templars' fortune, which remains undiscovered save in the overheated prose of fiction writers claiming to be historians.

While quack historians have used the Templar myth to sell books, major novelists of the late twentieth century provided a more respectable habitat for the monks: works of fiction. The great British novelist Lawrence Durrell in *Monsieur* drew on the equally fictitious writings presented as fact by von Hammer-Purgstall and Nicolai to link the Templars to Gnosticism and Ophitism. The inescapable Baphomet also pokes his head up in Durrell's novel. Thomas Pynchon's 1966 classic, *The Crying of Lot 49*, describes a secret society of Templars in contemporary America. The Italian novelist Italo Calvino found the medieval originals fodder for farce and lampooned their secret rituals while condemning them for a solipsism that blinded them to their eventual destruction.

A swashbuckling combination of power and tragedy, a morality tale that climaxed with trumped up charges of immorality, the story of the Knights Templars still fires the popular imagination, fascinating the reader with their genuine historical exploits as well as their legendary reincarnations.

The Templars are both a Rorschach inkblot and a mirror, often of the fun-house variety, reflecting the philosophy of their examiners rather than the subject. Over the centuries, they have been many things to many men. Their place in politics and polemics is so elastic they can be placed anywhere on the political spectrum to suit the needs of each political scientist and polemicist. Scholarly historiographers find them as irresistible as historical charlatans. The Templars remain as contemporary as a secret handshake between upper-crust twits who like to dress up in funny outfits and perform quasi-religious rituals. (Various members of Britain's royal family have headed the Masonic Templars in that country during the twentieth century.)

Long since departed from the scene—or have they?—these tonsured warriors continue to live on in legend and myth and cable TV documentaries.

Finding the truth will undoubtedly remain as elusive and impossible as, well, locating the Holy Grail.

BIBLIOGRAPHY

Addison, Charles G. *The History of the Knights Templars.* Kemtpon, Ill.: Adventures Unlimited Press, 1997.

Agrippa, Heinrich Cornelius ab Nettesheim. *Opera.* Lyons: 1533. Quoted in Partner 1990.

————. *De Occulta Philosophia Libri Tres.* Cologne: 1533. Quoted in Partner 1990.

Aroux, Eugène. *Dante Hérétique, Revolutionnaire et Socialiste.* Paris: J. Renouard, 1854.

Ashmole, Elias. *Institutions, Laws and Ceremonies of the Most Noble Order of the Garter.* London: 1672. Quoted in Partner 1990.

Baluze, Etienne. *Vitae Paparum Avenionensium.* Paris: 1693. Quoted in Partner 1990.

Barber, Malcolm. *The Trial of the Templars.* Cambridge: Cambridge University Press, 1998.

Barrow, John. *Life and Correspondence of Admiral Sir William Sidney Smith.* London: R. Bentley, 1848.

Barruel, Abbe Augustin de. *Memoirs Pour Servir a L'Histoire du Jacobinisme*. London: 1797–1798. Quoted in Partner 1990.

Baudouin, A. *Lettres Inedites de Philippe Le Bel* (*Memoires de L'Academie des Sciences, Inscriptions et Belles-Lettres de Toulouse*). 1886. Quoted in Barber 1998.

Bernard of Clarivaux, St. "*Liber ad Milites Templi de LaudeNovae Militiae,*'" in *Sancti Bernardi Opera*, ed. J. Leclerq. Rome: 1963. Quoted in Barber 1998.

Buc, George. "The Third Universitie of England," in John Stow, *Annales or a General Chronicle of England*. London: 1631. Quoted in Partner 1990.

Buonanni, Filippo. Ordinum Equestrium et Militarium Catalogus Imaginibus Expositus. Rome: 1711. Quoted in Partner 1990.

Burman, Edward. *The Templars Knights of God*. Rochester, Vt.: Destiny Books, 1986.

Cadet de Gassicourt, Charles Louis. *Le Tombeau de Jacques Molay ou Le Secret des Conspirateurs, a Ceux Qui Veulent Tout Savoir*. Paris: 1796. Quoted in Partner 1990.

Chacon, Alonso. *Vitae et Res Gestae Pontificum Romanorum et S.R.E. Cardinalium*. Rome: 1677. Quoted in Partner 1990.

Charpentier, Louis. *Les Mystères de la Cathédrale de Chartres*. Paris: R. Laffont, 1966.

———. *Les Mystères Templiers*. Paris: R. Laffont, 1967.

Clement IV. *Les Registres de Clement IV (1265–8)*. Paris: 1904. Quoted in Barber 1998.

Clement V. *Regestum Clementis Papae V ... Nunc Primum Editum Cura et Studio Monachorum Ordinis S. Benedicti*. Rome: 1885–1892. Quoted in Barber 1998.

Crowley, Aleister. *Magick without Tears*. Hampton, N.J.: 1954. Quoted in Partner 1990.

Curzon, H. de. *La Regle du Temple*. Paris: Libraire Renouard, H. Laurens, 1886.

De Bonneville, Nicholas. *La Maconnerie Ecossoise Comparee avec Les Trois Pressions et Le Secret des Templiers du 14e siecle*. Paris: 1788. Quoted in Partner 1990.

Del-Rio, Martin. *Disquisitionum Magicarum Libri Sex*. Cologne: 1679. Quoted in Partner 1990.

Dupuy, Pierre. *Traitez Concernant L'Histoire de France, Scavoir La Condemnation de Templiers*. Paris: 1700. Quoted in Partner 1990.

Fabre-Palaprat, Bernard Raymond. *Esquisse du Mouvement Heroique du Peuple de Paris dan Les Journees Immortelles des 26, 27, 28 et 29 Juillet 1830*. Paris: 1830. Quoted in Partner 1990.

———. *Levitikon, ou Expose des Principes Fondamentaux de La Docrtine des Chretiens Catholiques Primitifs*. Paris: 1831. Quoted in Partner 1990.

Favier, Jean. *Philippe le Bel*. Paris: Fayard, 1978.

Finke, Heinrich. *Papsttum und Untergang des Templerordens.* Munster: 1907. Quoted in Partner 1990.

Guillaume de Nangis. *Gesta Sanctae Memoriae Ludovici Regis Franciae,* in *Recueil des Historiens des Gaules et de La France,* ed. Bouquet, M. et al. Paris: 1738–1876. Quoted in Barber 1998.

Hammer-Purgstall, Joseph von. "*Mysterium Baphometis Revelatum.*" *Fundgruben des Orients:* 1818. Quoted in Partner 1990.

———. *Memoire Sur Deux Coffrets Gostiques du Moyen Age du Cabinet de M. Le Duc de Blacas.* Paris: 1832. Quoted in Partner 1990.

———. "*Die Schuld der Templer,*" *Denkschriften de Kaiserlichen Akademie dr Wissenschaften, Philosophisch-historische Classe.* Vienna: 1855. Quoted in Partner 1990.

Lambert, Malcolm. *Medieval Heresy, Popular Movements from Bogomil to Hus.* London: Edward Arnold, 1977.

Levi, Eliphas. *Histoire de La Magie.* Paris: G. Balliere, 1860. Quoted in Partner 1990.

Leys, A. M. "The Forfeiture of the Lands of the Templars in England," in *Oxford Essays in Medieval History,* ed. F. M. Powicke. Oxford: Clarendon Press, 1934.

Lyons, M. C., and D. E. P. Jackson. *Saladin: The Politics of Holy War.* Cambridge: Cambridge University Press, 1982.

Merzdorf, J. F. L. T. *Die Geheimstatuten des Ordens der Tempelherren*. Halle: 1877. Quoted in Partner 1990.

Michelet, Jules. *La Sorciere*. Paris: 1862. Quoted in Partner 1990.

———. *Histoire de France*. Paris: 1835–1867. Quoted in Partner 1990.

———. *Le Proces des Templiers*. Paris: 1841–1851. Quoted in Partner 1990.

Michelet, Victor-Emile. *Le Secret de La Chevalerie*. Paris: C. Bosse, 1930.

Mollat, G. *Les Papes D'Avignon (1305–1378)*. Paris: Letouzey & Ane, 1965.

———. *Lettres Communes de Jean XXII*. Paris: 1904-28. Quoted in Barber 1998.

Napoleon I. *Correspondance de Napoleon I Publie Par Ordre de L'Empereur Napoleon III*. Paris: 1858-69. Quoted in Partner 1990.

Nicholson, Helen. *Templars, Hospitallers, and Teutonic Knights: Images of the Military Orders, 1128–1291*. Leicester: Leicester University Press, 1993.

Nicolai, Friedrich. *Versuche uber die Beschuldigungen Welche dem Tempelherrerorden Gemacht Worden und uber dessen Geheimniss*. Berlin and Stettin: 1782. Quoted in Partner 1990.

Nodier, Charles. *Oeuvres Completes*. Paris: 1832–1837. Quoted in Partner 1990.

Nutt, Alfred. *The Legends of the Holy Grail*. London: D. Nutt, 1902.

Odo of Deuil. *De Profectione Ludovici VIII in Orientem*, ed. and tr. V. G. Berry. New York: 1948. Quoted in Barber 1998.

Paradin, Guillaume. *Chronique de Savoye*. Lyons: 1552. Quoted in Partner 1990.

Paris, Matthew. *English History from the Year 1215 to 1273*. London: Henry G. Bohn, 1852.

Partner, Peter. *The Knights Templar and Their Myth*. Rochester, Vt.: Destiny Books, 1990.

Perkins, C. "The Wealth of the Knights Templars in England and the Disposition of It after Their Dissolution," in *American Historical Review*, xv: 1909–10.

Raynouard, François. *Les Templiers, Tragedie*. Paris: Giguet et Michaud, 1805.

———. *Monumens Hisoriques Relatifs a La Condemnation des Chevaliers du Temple et a L'Abolition de Leur Ordre*. Paris: Impr. D'A. Égron, 1813.

———. "Etude sur 'Mysterium Baphometi Revelatum,'" *Journal des Savants*, 1819.

Runciman, Steven. *A History of the Crusades*. Harmondsworth: Peregrine, 1978. Quoted in Burman 1986.

Saint-Yves d'Alveydre, Joseph Alexander. *La France Vraie*. Paris: 1887. Quoted in Partner 1990.

Seward, D. *The Monks of War: The Military Religious Orders*. London: Eyre Methuen, Ltd., 1972.

Starck, Johann August. *Uber Die Alten und Neuen Mysterien*. Berlin: F. Maurer, 1782.

Strayer, Joseph R. *The Reign of Philip the Fair*. Princeton: University of Princeton Press, 1980.

———. *Medieval Statecraft and the Perspectives of History*. Princeton: University of Princeton Press, 1971.

Upton-Ward, J. M., ed. and trans., *The Rule of the Templars*. Suffolk, UK: Boydell, 1992.

Villani, Giovanni. *Selections from the First Nine Books of the Croniche Fiorentine of Giovanni Villani*, tr. R. E. Selfe and P. H. Wicksteed. London: 1896. Quoted in Barber 1998.

Voltaire. "*Des Conspirations contre Les Peuple ou des Proscriptions*" in *Nouveaux Melanges Philosophiques, Historiques, Critiques, etc.*, 1767. Quoted in Partner 1990.

Weston, Jessie L. *From Ritual to Romance*. Garden City, N.Y.: Doubleday, 1957.

———. *The Quest of the Holy Grail*. New York: Haskell House, 1964.

William of Tyre. *A History of Deeds Done beyond the Sea* (tr. by Emily Atwater Babcock & A.C. Krey). New York: Octagon Books, 1976.

Wright, Thomas. *A Discourse on the Worship of Priapus and Its Connection with the Mystic Theology of the Ancients*. London: privately printed, 1865.

INDEX

ABOUT THE AUTHOR

Nationally known author and syndicated columnist Frank Sanello has written over fifteen critically acclaimed books on history and film, including *The Opium Wars: The Addiction of One Empire and the Corruption of Another; Steven Spielberg: The Man, the Movies, the Mythology;* and *Reel v. Real: How Hollywood Turns Fact into Fiction* (the latter two published by Taylor Trade Publishing).

Sanello is currently writing *Faith and Finance in the Renaissance: The Rise and Ruin of the Fugger Empire,* a centuries-spanning epic about the influential family of bankers who were the German equivalent of their contemporaries, the Medici. Other forthcoming books of Mr. Sanello's include *To Kill a King: An Encyclopedia of Royal Murders and Assassinations from Ancient Egypt to the Present* and *Soap: A History of How the World Cleaned Up Its Act.*

A journalist for the past twenty-five years, Sanello has written articles for The Washington Post, The Los Angeles Times, The Chicago Tribune, The Boston Globe, The New York Times, and People, Redbook, Cosmopolitan, and Penthouse magazines.

Sanello was formerly the film critic for The Los Angeles Daily News and a business reporter for United Press International.

The author graduated cum laude from the University of Chicago and earned a master's degree from the University of California, Los Angeles, film school. He also holds a purple belt in Tae Kwon Do and has volunteered as a martial arts instructor at AIDS Project Los Angeles.

Sanello lives in Los Angeles with his four cats: Catullus, Cesare, Thisbe, and Pellegrino. He can be contacted at fsanello@aol.com.

OTHER TITLES OF INTEREST

Reel V. Real
How Hollywood Turns Fact into Fiction
Frank Sanello
240 pp., 29 b/w photos
0-87833-268-5
$19.95

SPIELBERG
The Man, The Movies, The Mythology
Updated Edition
Frank Sanello
304 pp., 34 b/w photos
0-87833-148-4
$17.95

Adam Clayton Powell, Jr.
The Political Biography of an American Dilemma
Charles V. Hamilton
576 pp., 36 b/w photos
0-8154-1184-7
$22.95

AGINCOURT
Christopher Hibbert
176 pp., 33 b/w illustrations, 3 b/w maps
0-8154-1053-0
$16.95

AMERICAN WOMEN ACTIVISTS' WRITINGS
AN ANTHOLOGY, 1637–2002
Edited by Kathryn Cullen-DuPont
656 pp., 17 b/w photos
0-8154-1185-5
$37.95 cloth

A BATTLE FOR THE SOUL OF NEW YORK
Reverend Charles Parkhurst's Crusade against
Police Corruption, Vice, and Tammany Hall,
1892–1895
Warren Sloat
440 pp. 30 b/w illustrations
0-8154-1237-1
$27.95 cloth

CITY UNDER SIEGE
Richmond in the Civil War
Mike Wright
376 pp., 15 b/w illustrations
0-8154-1220-7
$17.95

THE CIVIL WAR REMINISCENCES OF
General Basil W. Duke, C.S.A.
New Introduction by James Ramage
536 pp., 1 b/w illustration
0-8154-1174-X
$19.95

THE DELIGHTS OF DEMOCRACY
The Triumph of American Politics
Christian P. Potholm
200 pp.
0-8154-1216-9
$27.95 cloth

THE DREAM AND THE TOMB
A History of the Crusades
Robert Payne
456 pp., 37 b/w illustrations, 11 maps
0-8154-1086-7
$19.95

ESSAYS OF THE MASTERS
Edited by Charles Neider
480 pp.
0-8154-1097-2
$18.95

The Final Invasion
Plattsburgh, the War of 1812's Most
Decisive Battle
Colonel David G. Fitz-Enz
352 pp., 50 b/w illustrations
0-8154-1139-1
$28.95 cloth

GANDHI
A Biography
Geoffrey Ashe
432 pp., 18 b/w photos
0-8154-1107-3
$18.95

The Greenwich Village Reader
Fiction, Poetry, and Reminiscences, 1872–2002
Edited by June Skinner Sawyers
800 pp., 1 b/w map
0-8154-1148-0
$35.00 cloth

HAROLD AND WILLIAM
The Battle for England, 1064–1066 A.D.
Benton Rain Patterson
256 pp., 30 b/w illustrations
0-8154-1165-0
$25.95 cloth

HISTORY OF THE CONQUEST OF MEXICO & HISTORY OF THE CONQUEST OF PERU

William H. Prescott

1330 pp., 2 maps

0-8154-1004-2

$32.00

IMPERIAL SUNSET

The Fall of Napoleon, 1813–14

R. F. Delderfield

328 pp., 16 b/w photos

0-8154-1119-7

$18.95

THE LIFE AND TIMES OF MUHAMMAD

Sir John Glubb

416 pp., 12 maps

0-8154-1176-6

$18.95

MEMOIR

My Life and Themes

Conor Cruise O'Brien

488 pp., 27 b/w photos

0-8154-1064-6

$30.00 cloth

MEMOIRS OF MY LIFE AND TIMES
John Charles Frémont
696 pp., 89 b/w illustrations
0-8154-1164-2
$24.95

**ON CAMPAIGN WITH THE ARMY OF
THE POTOMAC**
The Civil War Journal of Theodore Ayrault Dodge
Edited by Stephen W. Sears
304 pp., 11 b/w illustrations
0-8154-1030-1
$28.95 cloth

ONCE UPON A TIME IN NEW YORK
Jimmy Walker, Franklin Roosevelt,
and the Last Great Battle of the Jazz Age
Herbert Mitgang
288 pp., 35 b/w photos
0-8154-1263-0
$16.95

THE SALEM WITCH TRIALS
A Day-To-Day Chronicle of a Community
under Siege
Marilynne K. Roach
656 pp., 11 b/w illustrations
0-8154-1221-5
$35.00 cloth

**THE SELECTED LETTERS OF
THEODORE ROOSEVELT**
Edited by H. W. Brands
624 pp., 4 b/w photos and illustrations
0-8154-1126-X
$29.95 cloth

SHORT NOVELS OF THE MASTERS
Edited by Charles Neider
648 pp.
0-8154-1178-2
$23.95

**THE SILENT AND THE DAMNED
THE MURDER OF MARY PHAGAN
AND THE LYNCHING OF LEO FRANK**
Robert Seitz Frey and Nancy Thompson-Frey
249 pp., 43 b/w illustrations
0-8154-1188-X
$17.95

THE SUNSET OF THE CONFEDERACY
Captain Morris Schaff
New introduction by Gary W. Gallagher
320 pp., 2 b/w maps
0-8154-1210-X
$17.95

T. E. LAWRENCE
A Biography
Michael Yardley
308 pp., 71 b/w photos, 5 maps
0-8154-1054-9
$17.95

TOLSTOY
Tales of Courage and Conflict
Edited by Charles Neider
576 pp.
0-8154-1010-7
$19.95

THE WAR OF 1812
Henry Adams
New introduction by Col. John R. Elting
377 pp., 27 b/w maps & sketches
0-8154-1013-1
$16.95

WOLFE AT QUEBEC
The Man Who Won the French and Indian War
Christopher Hibbert
208 pp., 1 b/w illustration, 4 b/w maps
0-8154-1016-6
$15.95

Available at bookstores; or call 1-800-462-6420

TAYLOR TRADE PUBLISHING
200 Park Avenue South
Suite 1109
New York, NY 10003